Happy Marriage:

A Christian Gal's Guide

To a Happy, Life-long Marriage

Leigh Ann Napier

Marriage Coach

Lexington, KY
www.ibloom.us

HAPPY MARRIAGE: A Christian Gal's Guide to a Happy, Life Long Marriage

Copyright © 2010 by Leigh Ann Napier

Published by iBloom
Lexington, KY 40555
www.ibloom.us

Requests for information should be addressed to:
iBloom, PO Box 55131, Lexington, KY 40555

Unless otherwise indicated, all Scripture quotations are taken from the HOLY BIBLE, NEW INTERNATIONAL VERSION®. NIV®. Copyright © 1973, 1978, 1984 by the International Bible Society. Used by permission of Zondervan. All rights reserved.

Verses marked with MSG are taken from The Message. Copyright © Eugene H. Peterson 1993, 1994, 1995, 1996, 2000, 2001, 2002. Used by permission of NavPress Publishing Group.

Verses marked NASB are taken from the New American Standard Bible®, © 1960, 1962, 1963, 1968, 1971, 1972, 1973, 1975, 1977, 1995 by the Lockman Foundation. Used by permission. (www.Lockman.org)

Verses marked NLT are taken from the *Holy Bible*, New Living Translation, copyright © 1996. Used by permission from Tyndale House Publishers, Inc., Wheaton, IL 60189 USA. All rights reserved.

Cover by Anna Quesada at Innovative Impulses.
www.innovativeimpulses.com

ISBN: 978-0-9826626-0-1

All rights reserved. No part of this publication may be reproduced, stored in a removal system, or transmitted in any form or by any means—electronic, mechanical, digital, photocopy, recording, or any other—except for brief quotations in printed reviews, without the prior permission of the publisher.

What others are saying...

"Happy Marriage will be a great resource to those who desire to build a strong foundation for their marriage and want a blueprint for learning the basics! Leigh Ann's honest relatable approach to the issues she addresses will draw you in without watering down the truth or over simplifying the message. If you are newly married or considering marriage, this will be a valuable tool for you. If you are a veteran at marriage, it will help you go back to the basics that we all need to depend on."

Sharon Wright, Elder & Lay Marriage Counselor

"I have witnessed Leigh Ann's heart to help women build lasting marriages first hand. You will find her insights biblical, refreshing, honest, and inspiring."

Glen L. Schneiders, Lead Pastor Crossroads Christian Church www.xroadschurch.org

"This book offers practical steps you can take to bless your marriage. It is entertaining and shares God's heart for a lasting, loving marriage. If you apply the principles in Happy Marriage, you are well on your way to many happy anniversaries! "

**Michael Smalley, M.A., Founder,
www.smalleyonline.com**

"Happy Marriage offers a terrific combination of humorous, light-hearted, thought-provoking stories with a large dose of Biblical TRUTH to offer women the punch needed to wake up and build their marriage on purpose! Our marriages are at risk today and since they are a KEY component in our witness to the truth of the gospel we ought to invest deliberately in them. Leigh Ann will help you to recognize your areas requiring attention and show you simple methods to move in a new direction. Written with grace in an easy-to-read, "girlfriend" style, this book is both a "giver" and a "keeper"!"

**Cristie Cerniglia, Contagious Ministries
www.contagiousonline.com**

"Leigh Ann is the greatest (and only) wife I've ever had!"

Mike Napier, wise and wonderful husband

A Happy, Life Long Marriage isn't for everyone. It will take a lot of prayer, hard work and determination. You'll have to zig when you feel like zagging many times but it will be worth it.

I recently heard a great definition of what separates winners from whiners:

"Winners do what is right and then feel good about it. Whiners want to feel good before they do what is right."
-John Maxwell

I want you to be a winner in your marriage, not a whiner. I want to help you move from being mastered by your feelings to being satisfied with your results.

I would love for you to join me in a Happy Marriage challenge: 7 Weeks to a Happier Marriage. Visit www.leighannnapier.com/7weeks to sign-up for this journey. This is a free resource to guide you through the material in this book and move you from just wanting a happy marriage to actually having a happy marriage.

As you take these tips to heart and incorporate them into your very own happy marriage, you will have success stories! Everything from, "I didn't bite my husband's head off for leaving the seat up even when I nearly fell in at 2am!" to "We are enjoying each other so much our friends are asking us what is wrong with us."

I would love to hear your stories! Please go to www.leighannnapier.com/hmstories and share your successes with me. Your story has the power to encourage another couple and we're all in this together, girlfriend!

Dedication Page

A Plea for Restoration of Marriage

"The exile survivors who are left there in the province are in bad shape. Conditions are appalling. The wall of Jerusalem is still rubble, the city gates are still cinders."

When I heard this, I sat down and wept. I mourned for days, fasting and praying before the God of Heaven.

I said, "God, God of Heaven, the great and awesome God, loyal to his covenant and faithful to those who love him and obey his commands. Look at me, listen to me. Pay attention to this prayer of your servant that I'm praying day and night in intercession for your servants; the People of Israel, confessing the sins of the People of Israel. And I'm including myself, I and my ancestors, among those who have sinned against you."

"We've treated you like dirt. We haven't done what you told us, haven't followed your commands and haven't respected the decisions you gave to Moses your servant. All the same, remember the warning you posted to your servant Moses: If you betray me, I'll scatter you to the four winds, but if you come back to me and do what I tell you, I'll gather up all these scattered peoples from wherever they ended up and put them back in the place I chose to mark with my Name."

"Well, there they are – your servants, your people whom you so powerfully and impressively redeemed. O Master, listen to me, listen to your servant's prayer – and yes, to all your servants who delight in honoring you – and make me successful today so that I get what I want from the king" (Nehemiah 1:3-11, MSG).

Oh God, we've made a mess of marriage. Men and women have made so many mistakes with the relationship design that you created. When I think of all of the divorces and broken marriages in our country today and in the past, my heart just breaks.

We've not followed your instructions, myself and my ancestors included. We deserve the mess we've made.

I call on you today, just as Nehemiah did. I call on you for my sake and for the sake of all those who love you and delight in honoring you. Not by my own name or my own merit, but on the trustworthiness of your promise to restore us when we come back to you and do what you tell us. Have mercy on us and help us to re-build marriage. Lord, we can't do it without you.

Contents

Introduction — 12

Chapter 1: **Avoid Expectations** — 19
- Check your attitude
- Show your gratitude
- Avoid comparisons
- Practice humility

Chapter 2: **Serve One Another** — 32
- You go first...don't wait for him to make the first move
- Pray for your spouse, asking God how you can help
- Ask your spouse what you can do for him
- Don't keep score

Chapter 3: **Remember To Be Friends First** — 48
- Encourage
- Listen
- Take up for him
- Enjoy

Chapter 4: **Share a Vision** — 61
- Write your dream list
- Share your dream list
- Prioritize your goals
- Help each other achieve them

Chapter 5: **Make Your Home a Safe Haven**   75
- Establish house rules for communicating
- Share a family calendar
- Provide breathing room
- Be intentional about your surroundings

Chapter 6: **Play Together**   91
- On dates
- While working
- At home
- In bed

Chapter 7: **Be a United Front**   106
- You must communicate
- Recognize scripture's instruction: WE not "YOU and ME"
- Come to a decision, then own it
- Have a "blind respect" for each other

Conclusion   120

My Happy Marriage Action Plan   124

Endnotes   129

Join in on the **Happy Marriage Challenge** by going to www.leighannnapier.com/7weeks. You will find a community of women who are on a 7-week journey toward making their desire for a Happy Marriage a reality.

Acknowledgements

This feels like my chance to give a speech at the Emmy's... I'll try to keep it short and sweet.

Thanks to my literature professor at Transylvania University, Ingrid Fields, my kindergarten teacher, Meredith Meade and all my teachers in between. You are amazing and wonderful and wherever you are today, thank you for investing in me.

Thanks to my husband, Mike, and my daughter, Halle Kate. You inspire me to want to be the wife and mom that God called me to be. I am so blessed and thankful to have you in my life. You are my joy.

Thank you Nanny (Aileen Sellards Hall) for writing poetry, weekly newspaper columns and for publishing 2 (soon to be 3) books of your own. You inspired me and planted the seed that I can do anything I put my mind to... including having a life-long marriage.

Thanks to Mom (Rhonda Hall Kretzer), not only for giving me life, braces and instilling a habit of good posture, but also for being the amazing mother and brilliant business-woman you are. You are strong and beautiful and resilient and I am forever thankful to you.

To Ken & Helen Napier, the best in-laws a girl could hope for.

To my mentor and friend, Cristie. Thank you for investing in me, encouraging me, believing in me, and for inviting me to Bible Study Fellowship. You are an amazing woman and your heart for God is truly contagious.

To my iBloom team: Kelly Thorne, Betsy Ringer, Tara McClenahan, Lori Burrell, Jane Thorne, Gena Sorenson...You are an amazing team of women and I am so privileged and blessed to work along-side you. An extra-special thank you to Nicole Webb & Sherry Shumate, iBloom Ambassadors of sorts, who have selflessly given their time, talent and energy to editing this book. I appreciate you all so much!

Lastly and mostly, thank you to God for showing me the importance of giving thanks in everything. Even when life is messy and our family tree is splintered, He can and will bring good out of what the enemy meant for evil. I am so thankful that He has given me a way to use my story to inspire and encourage others. God is good.

Introduction

No one wants a mediocre marriage. I doubt any of you went into marriage thinking, "This guy's ok, I think he'll do. We'll be roommates, split the bills, raise some kids, share our problems with each other, and have a boring sex life. Yep, that's what I want…a mediocre marriage."

NO! Statistically speaking, half of us grew up with over-the-top expectations of a fairy-tale life. Our parents' marriage wasn't perfect, but we grew up with it at least remaining in tact. We could take what they had made of their marriage and build our own to be even better. Then we were crushed when we got home from the honeymoon only to realize that our husbands weren't what we expected.

Then there's the other half of us who grew up seeing everything we didn't want to repeat (that is, if we ever did actually decide to take the plunge and get married in the first place). We knew everything NOT to do but lacked a vision of what TO DO for a strong committed loving marriage. For the months leading up to the wedding, we poured our hearts into creating the perfect wedding. That part we could control…the dress, music, food, favors. Done! Now what about the marriage itself? Not so much. We had vague expectations that we would do better than our parents had in love but we hadn't been able to define what that meant. For us, we are just happy to not be at each other's throats all of the time. If we make it to another anniversary and manage to avoid divorce, we're doing GREAT.

My personal story...

I am an Adult Child of Divorce (ACOD)[i] several times over. Divorce shook my family tree so hard that I decided to devote my life to helping marriages grow strong. To equip women for marriage and help them create a vision for marriage the way God intends it, not the way Disney confuses it or statistics doom it. After seeing the effects of divorce on so many in my own family and then experiencing what it feels like to be a child of divorce, I became compelled to be a part of the solution. I know just from the experience in my family and what I've learned so far in my own marriage that marriage as God intends it to be is broken. Happy, life-long marriages in our society have certainly become more of the exceptions in our culture than the rule.

In no way do I want to dishonor my parents in sharing this with you. I love them dearly and know that they have done the best they could given the experiences, the time they grew up in, and the information, expectations and preparation they had available. I'm not suggesting that they are perfect either. I'm sure they each played a part in what ultimately resulted in their divorce. My heart breaks for those of you who have experienced divorce or have witnessed someone close to you be devastated by it. Please know that I share my story for the sole purpose that God will bring beauty from ashes, believing in faith that he can and will restore that which the locusts have eaten (Joel 2:25).

My paternal grandmother was a victim of murder/suicide by her second husband. My biological father was 11 years old when he witnessed it. He and my mom were only married 2 1/2 years before they divorced; I was 6 months old at the time. I didn't see him again until I was 12 years old. Now we talk occasionally, but we rarely see each other even though we only live an hour apart.

Mom re-married when I was 2 and I was legally adopted by her second husband. They were married 18 years (during most of which they argued). I gained 2 sisters from their marriage and the man I know as "Dad". They divorced while I was away at college.

My mom re-married during my junior year at college and they are a great match. My step-dad is a great guy and they are really happy together. He was divorced twice before as well so we "joke" that the third time was a charm for them both. My legal dad says he'll never marry again. He had also been divorced before he married my mom. My biological father re-married and has been married for about 30 years now.

Relational deaths have stolen so much from me. I never met my paternal grandmother. I had a limited relationship with my paternal grandfather. The trauma that my biological father experienced is something that I will never fully understand. I feel such pain for him and that helps me to extend grace in knowing that he loves me the best way he can. I have to move forward thanking God for what He has given me, for the relationships I do have in my family and remembering that we will never fully understand why people love the way they do. I just remind myself that life has left scars on people. Some scars are more visible than others. Their scars have nothing to do with me but everything to do with the sin in this world. It is when I remember this that I am able to have a deeper love for Jesus who is love and truth; in Whom there is no darkness. I depend on Him to supply the only perfect love in my life. I hope you will realize this early in your marriage and remove the noose from your husband's neck... the rope that we tighten each time we are disappointed by our husbands. When we get married we are made one flesh and from then on when we cause harm, talk badly about, fail to pray for or fail to appreciate our spouse, the one we end up hurting the most is our self.

I share my story with you because I want you to know I can relate to what you may be going through and I understand if your view of marriage is a bit jaded. Divorce truly is a generational curse and I am determined to change my family tree. I want to help build healthy marriages, protect our children from the devastation divorce causes and glorify God with all that I do.

I'm so excited that you have picked up this book and that you have read up until this point! My prayer is that I can write God's truth in a manner that is well-received but not watered down. I challenge you to keep on reading. The title is Happy Marriage and now that we've gotten all of my family's divorce history out there, the remainder of this book will be focused on giving you the tools and information you need to build a happy, lasting, life-long marriage. There will be distractions to keep you from reading on; you will think of millions of things that you need to be doing rather than reading this book. You will feel your emotions taking over at times and think, well this may work for some marriages but it won't work in mine. I've seen too many couples start out in love only to end up in contempt for one another. That is the voice of the enemy. Don't listen to it! Refuse it. Don't underestimate God's ability to set a firm foundation for your marriage. There will be many things in life that will want your attention: children, work, friends, Church responsibilities, hobbies... But none of them should be placed in a higher priority than your marriage. God is first, marriage second, then children, and so on. When you get them out of order, it simply doesn't work.

    Your marriage has the ability to witness to others...and it will...one way or the other. It will either be a good example of marriage or a bad one: an example of Christ, serving one another in love or an example of two people constantly seeking to be served by the other one. Marriage is tough! No one (no one who's married anyway) will dispute that. Here's a visual for you. Have you ever been in a potato sack race? Marriage is a similar challenge: placing two people in a potato sack, i.e. marriage, and asking them to run the race of life together. From a human standpoint, you don't have a chance. There will be discomfort, conflict, confusion, clumsiness and exhaustion. Your flesh will be tempted to want to crowd the other person out or quit completely. But God instructs you to go against your feelings, your own understanding and instead make room for one more in that already-crowded potato sack. It is only if you invite a third person in that you will be able to finish the race.

You must invite Jesus into your marriage every day. You must ask Him for help in holding your tongue, giving you strength, changing your selfish attitude, giving you wisdom in ministering to your spouse; the list goes on and on. Remember that He is more than able to provide for you and your husband. He is excited when we realize that marriage is too big of a challenge to meet on our own. Many times it is when we become broken through this intimate relationship with our husband that we turn to Jesus for direction and comfort. He wants us to realize that we can't make it one day without His help. It is only after we recognize our absolute helplessness that we will wholeheartedly seek Him as our Savior.

Show God your fears about marriage. Show Him your weaknesses. Tell Him about the parts of yourself that want to stay on the top shelf of the closet, those things that you do not feel ready to share with Him or your husband. Tell Him how angry you are about your parents' divorce or the mess our world has made out of marriage today. He already knows these things. His heart grieves about them, too. So get it off your chest. You will feel so much lighter and He can then begin to work in your heart.

As you read this book, keep in mind that it and all marriage resources are absolutely useless on their own. This book does not have special powers to protect your marriage from destruction. There is no conference that will guarantee a 50th anniversary for you. Even the best premarital counselor in the world doesn't offer any guarantees. God's Word says "I am the vine and you are the branches. If you remain in me and I in you, you will bear much fruit; apart from me you can do nothing" (John 15:5). A fruitful marriage is one that is full of love, gentleness, peace, patience, joy, faithfulness, kindness, goodness and self-control. This is the fruit of the Spirit (Galatians 5:22). When we try to rely on ourselves, all we will end up with are sour grapes at best. When we are crazy enough to tell God, "I've got the hang of it now, God; I can do this marriage thing on my own." We are headed for TROUBLE! Recognize your complete dependence on Him for your breath, your life and your marriage. Give thanks for all that is good and ask Him for all you need each day. He will supply your needs but apart from Him, you can do nothing.

As you read each chapter, I challenge you to journal about your ONE TAKEAWAY that you will start to implement right away. Before moving to the next chapter, go to My Happy Marriage Action Plan beginning on Page 124 and pray that God will make it clear to you where he wants you to start. Then, do **ONE THING** to put what you've learned into action. For a guided journey through the book, visit www.leighannnapier.com/7weeks

Chapter 1

Avoid Expectations

Expectations can be toxic to a marriage. When we expect certain behaviors from our spouse and they fall short, we are disappointed. When we expect them to do something and they succeed, we take them for granted. Instead, practice showing appreciation for every act of kindness your mate shows you...whether that is taking out the trash or being a hard worker. Appreciate your mate.

❖ **Check Your Attitude:**

Have you heard the insane percentage of what is communicated non-verbally in relationships? I think it is something like 93% of what is communicated is done in a way other than the words we speak[ii]. That means that the message we are sending the world, our children and especially our husbands has little to do with the words we are using and almost everything to do with how we are delivering our message.

I bring this to your attention because I want you to be keenly aware of your attitude when you get up each day. Are you allowing yourself to be steered by your feelings? If so, you are in for a LOT of turbulence in life. We have to recognize that we are not mastered by our feelings... THANK YOU, GOD! Do you know what this can mean for your marriage? Do you know the amazing shift that occurred in my marriage when I really took this to heart?

When we have a bad attitude or our husbands have a bad attitude, we are bombarded by all of these feelings. Feelings that tell us what we want…NOW! Not tomorrow, not next week, or not even next year but what we want RIGHT NOW! I like to think of my feelings as my inner toddler throwing a tantrum and wanting candy for breakfast.

If we aren't careful to recognize our feelings and how they affect our attitude toward our life and toward our husbands, then these negative feelings can drive our relationships right over a cliff. God has given you full reign over your mouth. To go a step further, He has given you the choice in how you respond to everything in life. He has given you the ability to reject the temptation to act on those negative feelings and emotions. We have a choice.

It will be hard…I repeat, it will be hard… to go against our feelings when our spouse has disappointed us and we feel like saying something that isn't good. We may have even mastered the ability to remain silent rather than saying something we will regret. But that is only 7% restraint, isn't it? We have been given so many non-verbal communication tools and we know how to use them. There's the disapproving scowl, the agitated sigh, the "I know better than you do" eye rolling and the martyr syndrome of going about doing what we would normally do for our family but with a sour attitude. For example, closing doors just a little harder than necessary, making a dramatic performance out of emptying the dishwasher, talking to your child as a messenger when you are too angry to speak directly to your husband, just to name a few. How do I know these things so well? Because I have done all of them, of course.

My point is we do have a choice, every time, every day. We can choose to communicate life into our marriage, into our husbands, into ourselves. Or we can communicate death by being critical, pouty, playing a victim and being ungrateful. Whether you realize it or not, each day you are making a choice to either build up your marriage or tear it down. Your feelings, more often than not, will tempt you to tear it down. The enemy is SO GOOD at disguising these "feeling wolves" in sheep's clothing. We want to give into our "now" feelings for that instant gratification. Our feelings aren't thinking about our future. They want candy for breakfast. They are not on board with considering our long-term plans. They could care less about what happens to you next week. They just want what they want when they want it.

Do you know people like that? I do. They aren't good friends to have. They are there when they feel like it. They are there when it is convenient. They are there as long as they are getting something out of it. Once it gets tough or it fails to be fun, they are out of there. Those are not the kind of friends that I want to do life with. I want friends who will love me on good days and bad days. When I'm looking good and things are going well, but also on those days when I'm having a bad hair day and my skin has reverted back to its high school behavior and there's not enough concealer in the world to fix it.

So now that you may be realizing that you have gone too long without putting your inner toddler in time out, you may be wondering how you overcome those pesky feelings. How do you wake up with a bad attitude and then get up on the right side of the bed? How do you prevent those things that your spouse is doing that get on your last nerve from ruining your forecast for a bright sunshiny day in your relationship? Glad you asked, that leads us to the best attitude elixir there is: Gratitude.

❖ Show Your Gratitude

Have you ever noticed that it is nearly impossible to be angry or aggravated while you are being thankful? Think about it. When you are recognizing all that God has given you whether it is in prayer or journaling, you can feel your spirit being lifted. Your heart rate slows down. The wrinkle between your eyes relaxes. When thinking about all that you have rather than dwelling on all that you lack, a smile can proudly take back its territory on your face. You can't be all warm and fuzzy on the inside and want to go after your husband with a kitchen knife at the same time. The feelings have to fight for their position. If one is in, the other is out. The solution to a poor attitude is gratitude, plain and simple.

If your attitude toward your husband is critical, unloving and generally disappointed, I would almost guarantee that you have not spent time telling God how grateful you are for him and that you haven't told your husband thank you to his face lately either. Spend time in prayer thanking God for your husband. If you are having a hard time coming up with something to be thankful about, start by being thankful that God created him. If nothing else, tell God you are thankful that He isn't finished with your husband. Tell God you are thankful that you have someone to do life with, even if things aren't going as well as you had expected. Even if your marriage is feeling really tough right now, even if it seems you could not be more opposite from your husband if you had intentionally tried to marry your polar opposite, thank God for him - warts and all.

The next part might be easy for you or it might be difficult. Either way, do not skip this step. Make it a point to thank your husband for something at least 3 times a day this week. Now if you haven't done this in a while, he may look at you a little funny at first. That's OK. He may even think you are just being sarcastic. That's OK too. Rome wasn't built in a day. When you are genuinely showing gratitude toward your spouse, he will eventually feel the love and stop being suspicious that you just want something.

Don't let your thanks stop there. Make a habit of remembering and recognizing everything for which you are thankful. My friend and iBloom[iii] team member, Betsy Ringer, shared with me that she has a file on her computer dedicated to everything for which she is grateful. She adds to the list often and refers to it when she needs a boost. It is a folder on her desktop so she sees the little icon every time she gets on her computer. Set reminders like that around your home, too. You can have a journal filled with people, things and experiences for which you are grateful. You could keep messages on your refrigerator or post a sign in your laundry room that reminds you how lucky you are to have the clothes you are washing and the spouse/children who will wear them. Don't allow yourself to be pulled down by a bad attitude. Choose to live being grateful for each and every blessing God has given you and those you know you will receive one day. Have you read through your Bible? We win! That's enough to be grateful for, that alone.

- ❖ **Avoid Comparisons**

Comparisons can be gratitude killers. Avoid comparing your husband or your marriage to anyone else's. God has put you where you are and the grass is not greener on the other side. We are warned in scripture to not envy. Envy is poison to our heart and will kill your marriage.

This weekend we had family in town visiting. My daughter, Halle Kate, especially loved getting to play with her cousins, 4 month old Lucia and 2 year old Isabella. Halle Kate's attention span for Baby Lucia was pretty short but she would play with Isabella from daylight to dark. One of the issues, however, between a 2 year old and a 3 year old is that of sharing. It does not come naturally. They have to be taught that sharing is kind and that they will get their turn eventually. The two items of particular interest for them were a small red pasta cooker and a yellow shopping

Avoid Expectations

cart. If one had the pasta cooker then the other HAD to have it, too. Screaming, crying, tug of wars happened multiple times over the weekend. They envied what the other had. One minute they were fiercely competing for the pasta cooker, the next minute they were both trying to drive the cart. When I tried to offer the pasta cooker to convince one of them to let go of the cart, it didn't work. The pasta cooker had lost its charm. It wasn't envied anymore. It was old news.

Don't allow yourself to be fooled that your pasta cooker is any better or worse than your girlfriend's shopping cart. Your marriage is yours. When you compare it to someone else's, somebody always gets hurt in the process. And usually that person is you. It's great to have couples you admire or even couples who serve as mentors for you. What is not acceptable is when you allow your heart to step across the line and you begin to think or say things like, "I wish my husband did what hers does" or "I wish my husband was romantic like so and so." You can be sure that her husband does things that would get on your nerves and that he does plenty to get on her nerves.

There may be areas of your life that are tempting you to envy someone else's husband...maybe even to lust after a fictional character. If there are books you need to stop reading, television shows you need to stop watching, or friends you need to spend less time with, be willing to do these things. Scripture warns us that it is better to cut off our hand than use it to sin (Matthew 5:30). Sounds pretty drastic, doesn't it? I'm not asking you to amputate any part of your body, but I am asking you to consider the seriousness of the subject. Envy will poison your marriage and rob you of finding joy in your spouse. Be willing to cut things out of your life that aren't serving you, that don't build up your marriage or that aren't encouraging you to be the woman God wants you to be. It may hurt at first, but you will see God bless you for being disciplined in this area. Not to mention the example you are setting for your spouse and family.

Ask God to show you where you are making comparisons. Don't be fooled into believing that your husband has lost his charm or that he is old news. Ask God for help in breaking the habit of comparing your husband, your marriage, your house, your children or your life with others. For better or worse, your life is your life. Find a way to be grateful for it and entrust it to God. He is the only One who can make the necessary adjustments.

❖ Practice Humility

I once saw a quote on humility that explained it in the best way I had ever seen. The quote is: "Humility is not thinking less of yourself, but thinking of yourself less."- Michal Z[iv]. Isn't that it? It is not thinking you are less than, it is not allowing yourself to be trampled on or disrespected. It is simply thinking less about yourself in relationship to the time and energy spent on thinking of others.

Humility is especially important in your marriage. It is critical that both you and your husband shed your "me" mentality and replace it with a "we" mentality. The best way to achieve that shift of thinking in your marriage is for you to live it out. 1 Peter 3:1 tells of the power of a wife's actions in winning her husband to Christ and believing His word. "Wives, in the same way be submissive to your husbands so that, if any of them do not believe the Word, they may be won over without words by the behavior of their wives, when they see the purity and reverence of your lives." Don't ever underestimate the power of your actions when you are acting out of pure motives and you are practicing humility. I use the term "practicing" because we are all practicing humility. We will never perfect it. In fact, the moment anyone thinks they have "arrived" in humility, they have just lost it.

Even Jesus was tempted by the enemy to think of His own gain over God's plan for His life. In Matthew 4:8-11, Jesus is tested in the wilderness.

> "Again, the devil took him to a very high mountain and showed him all the kingdoms of the world and their splendor. 'All this I will give you,' he said, 'if you will bow down and worship me.'" "Jesus said to him, 'Away from me, Satan! For it is written: 'Worship the Lord your God, and serve him only.'"
>
> Then the devil left him, and the angels came and attended to him."

It will be very tempting during your marriage to want to think only of yourself, to want your own comfort above your spouse's and to want your spouse to meet your needs before you are willing to meet his needs. It will be tempting to think of yourself more and of your spouse less. But don't give in.

The enemy loves to disguise himself. He will lie to you and he will listen attentively to your self-pity. He will encourage you to think of all of the reasons your husband doesn't deserve you. He will help you take things your husband does and doesn't do for you and blow them out of proportion. He wants to mess with your perspective.

I'm reminded of a scene in a movie where a man drives off of a bridge and lands in the water. He manages to escape the car but then is so confused by what happened that he lost his perspective and swam down instead of up toward the surface. His loss of perspective in that situation was a matter of life and death. You will find that your ability to maintain a proper perspective in life and in marriage is also a matter of life and death. It was later explained that if you are faced with the situation of being disoriented under water, the way to regain your perspective is to look for bubbles and follow their direction. The bubbles will be floating up to the surface. Follow the bubbles. For your life, the bubbles we are looking for are found in God's Word. They are the life breathing Scriptures that instruct us. They help us to maintain or to regain our perspective. Without them, we will perish.

The enemy will want you to do things your way and he will offer you the world in exchange. For a while doing the wrong thing may make you feel better. Instant gratification, right? Serving yourself first, holding grudges, withholding kindness, being uncooperative...basically living out your "inner toddler's" instructions. Don't let the enemy fool you. John 10:10 warns, "The thief comes only to steal and kill and destroy; I have come that they may have life, and have it to the full."

Another Scripture I hold to when I am tempted to make a selfish choice or that I know isn't best for me or my family is Proverbs 14:12 "There is a way that seems right to a man, but in the end it leads to death." Do you know what this scripture is telling us? We will be confused at times, disoriented, tricked by the enemy. We will act, thinking we are making the right choice. Sometimes we are even willing to bet our life on it. But we can be dead wrong. Without looking to Scripture and praying for wisdom in our marriages, we won't have the proper perspectives and our marriages will sink.

Jesus gives us an example of what to do when we are tempted to let our self go to our head. When life becomes too much about "me, me, me", he gives us instructions about what to do. In John 6, after Jesus has just performed the miracle of feeding over 5,000 people with just 5 small barley loaves and 2 small fish, the people are completely amazed by Him. John 6:14-15 says, "After the people saw the miraculous sign Jesus did, they began to say, 'Surely this is the Prophet who is to come into the world.' Jesus, knowing that they intended to come and make him king by force, withdrew again to a mountain by Himself."

Jesus was surrounded by people who worshipped Him. He had just performed a miracle and this crowd was desperate for Him. Can you imagine how hard it would be to pull away from a crowd of more than 5,000 adoring fans? I don't know about you but I would be tempted to hang out there for a while and listen to them tell me how much they appreciated the amazing miracle I had just performed. But not Jesus, He recognized that they were tempting Him to become King before God's time. They adored Him for meeting their physical needs and they wanted more of their needs met by Him. In fear of losing perspective in the situation, He drew Himself away, alone, to a mountain. Now that is a statement.

When you are feeling sorry for yourself or you are thinking too much of yourself or you are being tempted to do something outside of God's will...run away to a place where you can be alone with God. Jesus knew He had to spend time alone with God in order to be refreshed and to regain the proper perspective. If you are finding it incredibly hard to act out humility in your marriage, go to the One who gave Himself freely for your sake, the One who was willing to wash the feet of the disciples, the One who died a criminal's death on a cross for all of us who didn't deserve it. Thankfully He did not wait for us to act first. He gave up everything for us before we even recognized Him or ever did anything for His sake. He thought of us more and of Himself less. Thank God He did.

Chapter 2
Serve One Another

We've all been there. We wait for the other person to make the first move. Or we start to feel sorry for ourselves because our hubbie doesn't do this or that for us. Stop it! The key to loving one another is to serve one another. You go first, every time, if necessary. Look for ways to be a blessing to your spouse and then follow through and actually do it.

"You, my brothers, were called to be free. But do not use your freedom to indulge the sinful nature; rather, serve one another in love" (Galatians 5:13).

Before you were married, your future mate was always on your mind. When you were together, you would wonder what he was thinking about. When you were apart, you were wondering what he was doing. If you saw anything, you would think of how it related to the love of your life.

You saw a bakery and thought "What is my Cupcake doing right now?"

At the grocery, "I wonder where we will eat on our next date."

If you listened to music, "I wonder if he is listening to the same station I am right now."

Before you met your mate, even if you were like me and thought you would be able to hold off getting married, these thoughts may have crept into your mind.

"I wonder:

- What he's doing right now?
- What he does for a living?
- What are his hobbies?
- What will he look like?
- When will we meet?
- Will I know for sure he's the ONE?

We were waiting with anticipation for this gift from God. We were longing for a mate. Someone to do life with, to love, depend on, to enjoy. We were devoted to the idea of him. Once we met, we were consumed with thoughts about the engagement. After getting engaged, we were buying all the bridal magazines (ok, I admit, I bought one BEFORE we were engaged… I was so nervous buying it; you would have thought I was shoplifting or something. I had a story ready that it was for a girlfriend just in case the clerk noticed that my ring finger was naked). Then we were consumed by the wedding planning, the honeymoon and then our home. Our husband got lost as we planned, planned, planned our life. He became an accessory for us. Kind of like how you need to take a kid with you to get into Chuck E. Cheese's. We needed this man to be "admitted" into this next phase of our life. Wedding, honeymoon, building a home together, having children, without him, we were kind of at a standstill.

I don't think any of us do it intentionally. I think we just get lost along the way. From the moment he asks us to marry him, we are swept up in the fairytale. The time we used to spend thinking about our spouse and how much we adored him and wanted him to be happy is replaced with one thing after another.

- Wedding
- Honeymoon
- Home
- Children
- Work
- Friends
- Church
- And on and on and on

It happens so quickly that we don't even realize it. We have to be intentional in putting a high priority on our spouse. Otherwise, something will always steal our time and energy and not leave much for him. You will both start to feel isolated from each other, even when you are in the same room. Without taking intentional steps toward each other, you will drift apart.

I remember going to the beach as a kid and riding a raft out into the ocean. I've watched enough shows about sharks with my husband now to never do that again. He is fascinated by sharks... I digress. As kids, my younger sister and I would take our rafts and just float around. We would have to keep an eye on where our hotel was, and where Mom and all of our things were. If we went too long without paying attention, we would drift so far down that we would lose our perspective. Then we would have to ride back in on the waves and walk to our starting point. Well, after a while, we wised up a bit. We would go beyond where Mom was before we even went back out in the water. We knew we were going to drift so we anticipated it. That way, when we got out of the ocean, we wouldn't be so far away and we could keep a closer eye on Mom and see her waving if it was time to go in.

When you serve your spouse, you are taking intentional steps toward him. You are keeping a priority on your husband. You are showing him that he matters. You will have things you have to do; you will have things you want to do. You will have a life apart from him, but don't lose sight of your partner while you are out on your raft. If you take your eyes off of him for too long, it will be hard to find him again. You'll have to do a lot more walking on the beach alone to get back to where you started…and that is if he is patient enough to wait for your return.

❖ You go first…don't wait for him to make the first move

By serving your husband, you are anticipating that drifting and you are compensating for it. The drifting can be because of something that you do, he does or that just happens to you both. Don't waste time and energy placing blame for the space between you. Just recognize it and take steps toward each other to correct it. And always be willing to go first.

Let's take a closer look at the scripture I mentioned earlier. Another translation puts it this way:

Galatians 5:13-15 (MSG)

> It is absolutely clear that God has called you to a free life. Just make sure that you don't use this freedom as an excuse to do whatever you want to do and destroy your freedom. Rather, use your freedom to serve one another in love; that's how freedom grows. For everything we know about God's Word is summed up in a single sentence: Love others as you love yourself. That's an act of true freedom. If you bite and ravage each other, watch out—in no time at all you will be annihilating each other, and where will your precious freedom be then?"

You may be just getting married, you may be still waiting for your wedding day or you may have been married awhile and have begun to lose sight of your spouse. Wherever you are, the best way to stay close to your spouse is to love your spouse. One of the best ways to love your spouse is to be willing to serve your spouse.

This reminds me of the quote, "The journey of a thousand miles begins with the first step." -Lao Tzu. Often that first step is also the toughest step to take. Don't allow it to be. If you find yourself being stubborn and not wanting to go first and thinking, "But I'm always the one who has to go first. Why should I have to go first all of the time? When is my husband ever going to serve me?" The first thing to recognize is that your inner toddler is speaking. Give her a sucker to shut her up. Then go to a quiet place and tell God about it. Pour your heart out to Him. He knows what you are thinking anyway so you might as well spill it. Let Him remind you that He is the only one who can shape your husband's heart. Let Him remind you that in serving others, you get more out of it than the one being served. He will remind you that He sees everything you do. Every time you respond in love. Every time you hold your tongue when you want to say something you shouldn't. Every time you give of yourself when what you really want is for someone to serve you instead. God sees it all, whether you can see any progress or not. Whether you think your husband even notices all you are doing, you are being sanctified. You are being changed, day by day, to be more like Christ. So whether your husband notices that you did 10 loads of laundry or you wiped the mess from the sink after he shaved or you cleaned out the science experiment that was growing in your fridge, isn't really the point anyway, is it?

- ❖ **Pray for your spouse, asking God how you can be of help**

    Remember that annoying thing I mentioned earlier? That God is the only one who can change your husband's heart? You may have skimmed right on by it. I know I did for a couple of years in my marriage. I wasted a lot of time and energy thinking I could do something about his heart. I would post inspirational quotes on the fridge, leave books on his nightstand, encourage (nag) him to join a men's Bible Study at Church.

You see, I tried to take on something that was not my responsibility. I tried to take on the mission to mold my husband's heart. That is not my job. No amount of nagging in the world will make my husband the man God created him to be. In fact, the more I tried, the more resistance I felt. My husband is an amazing man. He's a believer. We've always gone to church together. He doesn't need fixing. I just thought... (Those can be dangerous words from a wife's mouth in regard to her husband. You can guarantee some rationalization is following close behind them.)

I just thought...

- He wasn't doing enough
- He wasn't maturing spiritually as fast as I wanted
- He wasn't reading enough marriage books
- He wasn't reading enough parenting books
- He didn't have enough strong Christian friends
- He wasn't romantic enough
- And on and on and on.

Stop it! Wasted time, wasted words, wasted energy. I just thought that I could change him. I just thought that I knew better than he did. I just thought God wasn't doing enough in my husband's life. I just thought that I needed to parent my husband.

Sounds ridiculous but so many women do just that. They parent their husbands. They tell them what to do and when to do it. They make the decisions and then fill them in on a "need to know" basis. They are too busy bossing them around to know what their husbands are thinking. They are so concerned with being in control of everything that they miss out on the joy of being partners in marriage. No wonder so many women become angry, frustrated, tired, lose their sexual appetite and become resentful toward their spouse. They are taking on responsibilities that don't belong to them.

God's Word tells us this: "If you are tired from carrying heavy burdens, come to me and I will give you rest. Take the yoke I give you. Put it on your shoulders and learn from me. I am gentle and humble, and you will find rest. This yoke is easy to bear and this burden is light" (Matthew 11:28-30, CEV).

A yoke is something that is put on the necks of animals for plowing. With a yoke on their shoulders, they are able to pull a wagon or plow a field. In Jesus' day, people were familiar with the symbol of a yoke. They knew that a yoke represented hard work and obedience. Another translation says it this way. "Are you tired? Worn out? Burnt out on religion? Come to me. Get away with me and you'll recover your life. I'll show you how to take a real rest. Walk with me and work with me - watch how I do it. Learn the unforced rhythms of grace. I won't lay anything heavy or ill-fitting on you. Keep company with me and you'll learn to live freely and lightly" (Matthew 11:28-30, MSG).

There is so much that can be applied to marriage from this passage that I don't know where to start. Jesus is wise beyond my brain's capacity to take it in. And yet still, I often get stuck thinking that I know more about my life than He does. I know I'm not alone in this...

First, Jesus asks us if we are tired. Today, I could hear a friend asking me, "So, how's that working for ya? Looks like you could use a little help." Then we would have to admit that what we are doing isn't working out the way we thought it would. We need help.

Next, Jesus tells us what to do once we realize (or in many of our cases, we just stop long enough to remember) that Jesus is, in fact, smarter than us. He doesn't do this in an arrogant way, but in a loving way. I see Him looking at me like I look at my 3-year old when she is trying to get her shirt on. Sometimes she does it easily. Other times, she will try to put her head in the armhole and get stuck; and she will be so determined to do it on her own she won't let me help. I just wait there, knowing that sooner or later, she will ask for my help. Halle Kate is pretty stubborn so I know I could be there awhile. I'm not going to get angry with her or bully her or lecture her that I am better at getting her dressed than she is. Of course, I'm better at it. I'm 33 and she's 3. Well, Jesus knows that He is the wise one, that His ways are THE way, and that in the end, we need Him above all else. After all, He is our Creator and we are merely human. But He also won't make us come to Him. He waits patiently for us to realize we need Him and then He is there in an instant. Actually, He never left.

After we come to Him, after we have realized our great need for Him, He adjusts our load. He makes our tasks manageable again. He gives us a custom-made yoke, designed just for us. He asks us to walk with Him and learn from Him. He doesn't ask us to run ahead of Him. He doesn't say we have to run to catch up with Him. He meets us where we are and asks us to walk with Him and learn as we go.

If we get too far ahead of ourselves, we become anxious. If we stay with Jesus, moment by moment, He will show us how it is done. He will make our burden lighter and easier to bear. I love the last part of The Message translation above, "Keep company with me and you'll learn to live freely and lightly."

So, how do you "keep company" with Jesus? By spending time in His Word and in prayer. How do you know when you are getting ahead of Him or falling behind? When you become tired, worn out, when you are taking on burdens that do not fit you. Like trying to parent your husband or make all of the decisions in your household or when you are not willing to help your husband.

Many women are afraid of the yoke in marriage. They are filled with wrong thinking and afraid they will be taken advantage of. They have had bad experiences or they have seen other women who were abused or neglected or abandoned. I challenge you to look at this in a new light. I'm not asking you to take on your husband's yoke. Jesus doesn't ask you to take on your husband's yoke. Jesus asks us to take on His yoke. We can trust Him with our lives. There is no need to fear what Jesus gives us to bear. If you are feeling like you are working and working and working in your marriage and you aren't seeing any results, ask Jesus to show you what you are taking on that is not yours. Spend time in prayer and learning His word. Allow Him to teach you how to live freely and lightly, not just in your marriage, but in all areas of your life. God is the only one who knows what is best for your husband. Get on board with His plan. Ask God what He wants for your husband and how you can help. Your marriage, your husband and your life will be blessed for it.

❖ **Ask your spouse what you can do for him**

Now that we have learned to leave nagging in the past, take the first step in becoming the most amazing wife on the planet. Ask your husband what you can do to help him. Sounds easy, huh? Yet there are SO MANY wives who never ask their husband this question. Here are a few reasons wives don't ask:

- I'm already so busy; I can't add more to my plate.
- He may want me to do something I don't want to do.

- He may want me to do something I don't know how to do.
- He will take advantage of my niceness.
- I won't have any time for me if I offer to help him.
- He hasn't offered to help me, so why should I help him?

In marriage, we are called to serve one another. We need to get past whatever is preventing us from asking our husbands if they need help. The underlying reason we don't ask our husbands how we can help them is fear. Fear of it being too much, fear of being used and fear of being unappreciated. The Bible has a lot to say about fear. The cliff note version is to get rid of it and do not make any decisions because of it.

Isaiah 43:1 instructs us to put off our spirit of fear, "Fear not, for I have redeemed you; I have summoned you by name; you are mine." The Message explains Isaiah 43:1-4 as:

> "When You're Between a Rock and a Hard Place
>
> But now, God's Message, the God who made you in the first place, Jacob,
> the One who got you started, Israel:
> 'Don't be afraid, I've redeemed you.
> I've called your name. You're mine.
> When you're in over your head, I'll be there with you.
> When you're in rough waters, you will not go down.

> When you're between a rock and a hard place,
>   it won't be a dead end—
> Because I am God, your personal God,
>   The Holy of Israel, your Savior.
> I paid a huge price for you:
>   all of Egypt, with rich Cush and Seba thrown in!
> That's how much you mean to me!
>   That's how much I love you!
> I'd sell off the whole world to get you back,
>   trade the creation just for you.'"

I don't know about you, but for me, that puts things in the proper perspective. I'm afraid that if I run this errand for my husband that I'll be taken advantage of. God's Word says fear not because I belong to Him. Even if I find myself in a tough situation as a result of serving my husband, God has my back. His Word says that He would give up everything and has given up everything through His son Jesus, for me. Even if it had just been to save only me, He would have done it. So what do I have to be afraid of?

I am convinced that in marriage, God is asking us to trust Him. He is asking us to trust our husbands, to a degree, but mostly He is asking us to trust Him. He wants us to serve our spouse. He wants us to be willing to step out of our comfort zone. He wants us to believe that whatever we encounter, we will overcome it with Him. John 16:33 reminds us that "In this world you will have trouble. But take heart! I have overcome the world." If we trust that Jesus has really overcome the world, that He is with us, that we have His Spirit living inside us, then how can we allow ourselves to be fooled by the enemy into thinking that if we make ourselves available to helping our husbands, we are somehow doomed? It is nonsense and it is a marriage killer. Husbands need their wives. We are a part of God's plan to make him the man he is destined to become. We can choose to be available to God and to our husbands in making those plans a reality or we can choose to live in fear and miss out on what God has called us to do.

❖ Don't keep score

The next temptation after we have gotten on board with God's plan and we are making ourselves available to help our husbands is to want to keep score. I did this for him, now it is his turn to do this for me. Or I cooked Monday and Tuesday so tonight it is his turn. Or, I gave him a fantastic birthday present so he'd better deliver this year for my birthday. I think what is at the heart of the issue when it comes to keeping score is the topic of MOTIVE. What is our motive in serving our husband? Is it to get recognition? Is it to be served in return? Is it to store up deposits with our husbands so we can make withdrawals when we want? Are we serving because we want something?

We're human so more than likely we serve for all of these reasons and then some. But that does not make it right. Our motive for doing something is incredibly important to God. He wants us to make our inner toddler grow up. He understands why we tend to serve with selfish motives but he wants us to get rid of that ugliness in our hearts. He wants to sanctify us, i.e. make us more and more like Jesus Christ every day. Jesus didn't have a selfish bone in His body. When we serve with selfish motives, in Jesus' eyes, we have missed the point. When we serve because we know that is what God calls us to do, regardless of what we get in return, we are becoming more like Jesus.

Nothing you do is missed by God. He sees every time you choose to serve in love rather than retaliate in selfishness. He promises that we will give an account of our lives, that we will receive a great reward one day. We are not responsible for our husband's response to our faithfulness. We are only responsible for our obedience to what God has called us to do.

If you are having a hard time with this serving your husband thing, ask God to search your heart and make it clean. I once heard a speaker say that if God's Word is offensive to you, then you need to take that up with God. It isn't His Word that is causing the problem. It is your heart. Something has gotten lost or mixed up or perverted in translation. Ask Him to show you His heart. When we look to Jesus as our example and realize that keeping score is not something He does with us, it makes it much easier to serve for the sake of serving. It makes it easier to trust that God is working on your husband's heart and on your behalf. If you happen to see results right away and your husband recognizes you for the princess you are, that is a bonus, my dear. Do not expect it every time. Just use it as a reminder to show your gratitude to Jesus for loving us when we do not appreciate Him and for giving His life for us when we have no way of paying Him back. In fact, scripture tells us that the best we have to offer Him is like filthy rags (Isaiah 64:6). It has been likened to the cloths that women used as sanitary pads back in the day. That's a humbling thought.

What is your ONE TAKEAWAY that you will start to implement right away? Before moving to the next chapter, go to My Happy Marriage Action Plan beginning on Page 123 and pray that God will make it clear to you where he wants you to start. Then, do **ONE THING** to put what you've learned into action. Reminder: for a guided journey through the book visit www.leighannnapier.com/7weeks

Chapter 3

Remember To Be Friends First

Friend: One attached to another by affection or esteem.[v] Yep, that sums that up. Even if you aren't feeling particularly friendly, still act toward your husband like you would with a friend. Many couples are more hateful towards each other than they would ever consider being with a close friend. Your mate is the other half of your body, handle with care.

Think of your favorite friendship. What qualities does it have? What do you enjoy most about that relationship that you have formed? What do you do together? Why do you like this person? Now, take a minute and think about what they would say about you and the friendship they have with you. What qualities would they say they most appreciate about you?

Now, after you have thought that over a bit, after you have considered what friendship looks like to you, would you say that you are a good friend to your husband? Would you say that he is a friend to you? Many people would argue that their spouse is not very friendly toward them. I would argue that the best way to have a good friend is to BE a good friend first.

I think many people are using the word "friend" too lightly today. There is a difference between a friend and an acquaintance. You see an acquaintance is someone you recognize and someone who would recognize you. A friend is someone for whom you are willing to step out of your comfort zone. A friend is someone you let in. They know you aren't perfect. You know they aren't perfect. You offer mercy and grace to one another. You believe the best about each other. You make allowances when one of you is having a bad day. You take up for each other. You don't let others talk badly about your friend. And of course, YOU don't talk badly about your friend to others. You tell each other the truth. You will even risk hurting their feelings if it will protect them from a bigger hurt: like wearing a horrible outfit or if their hair color is all wrong or if their breath stinks. You share these things with each other bravely but always in love.

How many women do you know who don't offer the same courtesies to their husbands? Have you been one of those women? Whether you've been a friend to your husband up until this point or not, there is always room for improvement. By learning the art of cultivating friendship with your spouse, you can be an ambassador for marriage.

❖ **Encourage**

One of the best ways to be a friend to your man is to encourage him. This will require that you show an actual interest in him. For some of you this is easy, for others it will have to be a learned behavior. Either way, a great starting point, as I mentioned, is to show interest in the things that interest him. It is hard to encourage someone when you don't know their interests, their dreams and their insecurities. If you don't know these things about your husband, ask him. Don't ambush him with an hour-long interview but instead weave in some questions over dinner or at night before you both go to sleep.

It is so easy to get caught up in what you do with each other as a couple and lose sight of what drew you to each other in the first place. If you are asking questions, showing genuine interest in what he is facing, encouraging him in his interests and offering support for those areas where he feels threatened or insecure, then you are well on your way to being his best friend. As you offer encouragement to your spouse and you continue to pray for him, get ready for God to do big things in your husband's life.

Men often measure themselves by their success. If their job seems like it is headed for a dead end or if they just haven't achieved anything that they would deem significant, they can find themselves in a "man funk". You, as his encouraging wife, have the power to bring him up out of it. Through prayer and encouragement, you can get your husband excited about life. You can build him up and you can partner with God in bringing the plans for his life to pass. Don't ever underestimate the value of your encouragement toward your husband.

One thing to caution you about before moving on: don't allow yourself to fall into the habit of criticizing your spouse. Will he do things wrong? Yes! Will he drive you nuts at times? Absolutely! But don't allow his behavior to be confused with his identity. If he leaves his shoes on the floor and you are constantly tripping over them, keep the subject on the shoes.

Bad example: "You always leave your shoes lying around and I nearly killed myself tripping over them again. How can you be so insensitive?!?"

Good example: "I think your shoes have it out for me. I nearly killed myself when I tripped over them this morning. Could you please put them in the closet next time?"

You get bonus points if you can manage to maintain your composure and add some humor to the conversation. Sometimes there are things that you and your husband will do habitually and there is not much hope that these behaviors will change. This could be a quirk of personality differences, one neat and tidy; one who doesn't see the mess. If that is the case, then find a way to make it work without tearing each other apart. Choose to extend grace even if you are doing it through clenched teeth. It is better to do that than to say hurtful things since your husband was not doing something with the intent to hurt you in the first place. After all, I'm sure you do some things that drive him crazy too, and not in a good way.

Consider this scenario. You come to a 4-way stop. It is your turn to go but you see this car coming at a high speed. You can choose to go, since it is, in fact your turn, or you can wait and exert caution until the speeding car passes. If you wait, you make it to live another day. If you choose to go to prove your point or to stick to your principle, you may be right but you will be DEAD right. Meekness is defined as strength under control. It is having the power to crush someone's spirit or to say something hurtful or to kick someone while they're down, but deciding to reserve your strength out of mercy for the other person. You will have plenty of ammunition as you learn more and more about this man you have married. My prayer is that you will always use your strength with caution. You will overcome your flesh's desire to be dead right.

It may not mean he will be promoted to president or that he will win millions of dollars, but when he feels and knows his wife is believing in and praying for him, he will feel like a million bucks.

❖ Listen

This could be one of the most important communication tools in your marriage: Listening. You would think it would be something that comes naturally. After all, you are not actually DOING anything while you are listening, right? Wrong. Listening is hard to do. Here are just a few reasons[vi] why it is so hard to be a good listener.

- People tend to talk much slower than we are thinking. So while they are pouring their heart out, we are already mentally on to something else.
- We only retain approximately 25% of what is being said. On average, people can only recall 17.2% of the news they just watched. At best, no one did better than 25%.
- We are overscheduled. Listening takes time and we have already planned out each minute of our day, sometimes double booking ourselves. How many of

us have put "Listen to my spouse" in our planner? We are multitasking as we listen.

There have been so many times that I have called friends and we talk back and forth. Sometimes I catch a friend in a crisis moment. I will take the next half hour to just hear what is going on in their life. I have not said much of anything, just "yes, uh-huh, and really" so she wouldn't think we had gotten disconnected. It is at the end of those calls that my friend feels most understood. She feels closest to me. She thinks I'm fantastic. And I did not feel like I had done anything. But really I had. I listened.

Women have a lot more daily "word currency" than men. James Dobson wrote in his *Focus on the Family* column, June 2004[vii]:

"Research makes it clear that little girls are blessed with greater linguistic ability than little boys, and it remains a lifelong talent. Simply stated, she talks more than he does. As an adult, she typically expresses her feelings and thoughts far better than her husband and is often irritated by his reticence. God may have given her 50,000 words per day and her husband only 25,000. He comes home from work with 24,975 used up and merely grunts his way through the evening. He may descend into Monday Night Football, while his wife is dying to expend her remaining 25,000 words." This, more often than not gender difference, tells me two very important things to consider as it relates to marriage:

Happy Marriage

1. When your husband says something, drop everything and listen because he will not speak nearly as often as you and he probably is trying to make himself heard or he needs your help. Try to savor it because he is spending his precious word currency on you.

2. You NEED to have girlfriends! We have oodles and oodles of word currency and it is burning another hole in our mouths!!! (So to speak.) In order to get those words out each day and not grow furious with our husbands for not responding to even a third of the words we say, we need to talk it out with our girlfriends. I would caution you to keep the girl talk wholesome, allow no room for gossip among you, and of course, don't trash-talk your spouse. We covered that already but I thought it would be a good thing to mention again, just in case you were not listening earlier.

Just by taking the time to listen to your mate, he will feel closer to you, understood by you and supported by you. Please resist the urge to answer the phone, run the vacuum, walk on the treadmill or catch up on your DVR recordings while he is trying to spill his heart out to you. Those things will still be there after you have heard him out and chances are you will not have to listen for too long.

❖ Take Up For Him

If you haven't noticed, women who disrespect their spouse in front of others are a hot button of mine. I will never forget going on a double date years ago with another couple. Throughout the entire dinner she made one jab after another toward her husband…right in front of us! That was one time the check could not come fast enough. My husband and I were both very uncomfortable and we felt bad for the guy. The saddest part is that he didn't even seem to notice it. This made us think the behavior had been going on in their relationship so long that it didn't even show up on his radar anymore. Plus, if she was that disrespectful in front of others, we did not want to know what was said behind closed doors, or when she was out with girlfriends.

You and your spouse should establish early on in your relationship that you are on the same team. You may have disagreements about things. You will not always see eye to eye. Some things you will decide to just agree to disagree on. But never allow that to come between you in a way that you are the adversary of your spouse. Here's where that "One Flesh" reality comes back in a big way. You should protect your spouse as you would your own body. If someone is speaking poorly about him, take offense. Be the first to point out his strengths. Change the subject. If it is your spouse who is down on himself, encourage him. Remind him of all of the things you love about him. Remind him of why you married him. Remind him of who he is in Christ.

In Extreme Circumstances...

A Word of Caution:

If there is any abuse going on, get professional help with a counselor or a leader in your Church. Love should not hurt and you are not bound to a relationship that is abusive. Get out, be safe and consult a professional in weighing your options going forward.

If the issue is not one of physical or emotional abuse but you are encountering problems, resist the temptation to talk negatively to your friends or parents about him. That will cause more harm than good. Their emotions and allegiances to you can get in the way. They may take sides without giving godly counsel. If you were just having a misunderstanding and you end up reconciling, your friends and family may find it hard to welcome him back into their hearts. They may forever hold a grudge against him. More often than not, when we are in a situation where there is conflict, we are heavy on discussing our spouse's faults and light on sharing our part in the problem. I've seen friendships broken over these conflicts and family members forever tense about them long after you and your husband have resolved the squabble.

- ❖ **Enjoy**

The last tip on the topic of cultivating friendship with your spouse is to make an effort to enjoy your spouse. What a concept, right? Believe it or not, without being intentional in this area, it is possible for you to wake up next to him one day and wonder what you ever saw in this guy. If you are not purposely drawing closer together, you will unknowingly drift apart.

Here are some ideas to get you thinking in terms of enjoying your spouse. For some of you this may come easily. Others may find this extremely hard. You may be thinking, "With work and kids, I just don't have the time or the energy to think of ways to enjoy my spouse. We'll enjoy each other after the kids move out or when we retire." Scrap that thinking. If you don't take the time and set aside enough energy to enjoy your spouse along the way, there may be nothing left for you to enjoy when the kids are not home to hold you together. You could divorce or one of you could get hit by a bus. I know, harsh words coming from a hopeless optimist, but I really want you to get this concept. We are not promised tomorrow. We have only been given the gift of today. So if something has to be sacrificed now so that you will have the time and energy to enjoy your spouse today, then do it. Watch less television, forego the book club, don't sign your kids up for every activity under the sun. Protect the enjoyment of your spouse like a mother bear protects her cub. Fight fiercely for the time and energy it will require.

For you moms or future moms reading this, grab your highlighter, an index card, whatever it takes for you to remember this: the best gift you can ever give your children is a solid, secure relationship between their mother and their father. Do not sacrifice that security in exchange for karate lessons. There is nothing wrong with allowing your child to be involved in activities. Just be sure that the child is aware that your relationship with your husband is a higher priority than a parent's availability as taxi driver. Your spouse comes first, then your child. Your commitment to your spouse was designed by God to last a lifetime. Your relationship with your children is for the purpose of training them to grow up, leave home and get married themselves. You are training them to be able to be responsible adults. Your goal is to get them to leave you. I know that is like a dagger to your heart. Take it up with God, not me. The goal for your marriage is for no one to leave anyone. Trust it to God, do not become a control freak. I just want you to recognize the difference. Your spouse is your partner before, during and after the parenting years. Do not put your marriage on hold while you raise your children and then expect to be able to pick up where you left off once your child is ready to fly the coop.

So, now that you've creatively cleared your schedule, what to do with your spouse? I have a great suggestion. Go have sex.

God dedicated an entire book of the Bible to sex. Did you know that? I think I was 30 years old before I knew that. They never taught me about it in Sunday school. I had to go and check the Bible that I had had forever just to see if Mom had cut it out or something. I had never heard of this book called Song of Solomon. The entire thing is about the joy of sex. No wonder while growing up my preacher never had me memorize any of those verses in Vacation Bible School.

Thankfully, more and more churches are willing to talk about and even encourage sex. We have allowed the secular society to make sex into something it isn't. They have made it cheap, diseased, and anything but exclusive. They have used it more for the purpose of selling stuff than for its intended purpose. God created sex for a husband and wife to enjoy each other and to create adorable mini-people. How we have managed to mess it up so much I may never know. So there, that is a great way to start enjoying your husband more. Go have sex! Too tired? Go get some sleep and then enjoy sex. Not feeling frisky? Do what lovers do until you feel like lovers feel. Go have sex.

Now what if your husband is all about himself when it comes to sex and it has not been fun for you? First, shame on him. Second, shame on you because men are pretty much clueless when it comes to what makes you happy in bed. Heck, we don't even know what makes us happy in bed a lot of the time. So don't be shy in giving your husband some clear directions. If you do not speak up, you are going to miss out on one of life's greatest pleasures. This is SO worth getting right. Do not give up after just a few tries either. God made your body and more likely than not, you are physically capable of enjoying sex. It just takes patience and persistence, and a little Astroglide never hurt anyone either. I'm just saying...

There is an exception to the practice makes perfect advice. As I mentioned earlier, our world has really messed up sex as it was intended. This means, not only that we have mixed messages, but that many of you have been abused, raped and some have real physical problems that prohibit you from enjoying sex. If you or your spouse is suffering from any type of sexual dysfunction, put down this book and go set an appointment with a counselor and/or doctor. This will take time and godly counsel to get you to the point of enjoying sex as the gift God created it to be. Do not be afraid to reach out for help.

Chapter 4
Share a Vision

So what is it that will keep you both going when times are tough, or life is hard or when you both are just tired? What is it that will keep you connected and in love and faithful to each other 'til death do you part? What is it that will keep your feelings from taking over and wrecking your ship? One word: Vision.

You see it is so easy to give in to your feelings. To not feel like serving your spouse or to not feel like remaining faithful to each other or to feel fed up with the way your life is going during a season. You have to have an anchor and in this case, a future anchor. Your vision is an anchor that is ahead of you, drawing you both forward. Keeping you both moving toward it and preventing you from going off in separate directions. You need a vision for your life and you need a vision for your marriage.

I have been blessed with the best grandparents in the world. Some of my best memories growing up were spent on boats. My grandparents owned a boat store named Hall Marine. When I was little, I spent a lot of time with my family on the lake. I have wonderful memories of Nanny cooking delicious meals; Pop teaching me to fish; and Mom and I just enjoying time together. Most of the time, we were content to just keep the houseboat at the dock and it was still an adventure. But sometimes, Pop would make it a point to venture away from the dock; Nanny would make a special dinner and my all-time favorite houseboat treat, her virgin frozen pina coladas. Pop would find just the right spot on the lake for us to stop and enjoy dinner. He knew the lake well and after years of fishing, he had many spots that were his favorites. Once we arrived, he would drop anchor. That anchor would keep us in the right spot and allow us to really enjoy our dinner without worrying about running into something or going too close to shore and grounding the boat. The anchor allowed us to not stress out over our location while we enjoyed a relaxing meal.

On the lake, our boat had a physical anchor. For each of us on that boat, sharing common interests and love for each other served as an anchor for our lives. My grandparents had to do a lot of work to make those visits so special for me. My grandparents were hard workers. They worked hard so they could play hard. Aside from all that it took to have a houseboat to visit, just preparing for that day at the lake took preparation. My grandmother had to have the kitchen supplied with all of the pots, pans, plates, cups, utensils and napkins. She had to go to the store to get all of the ingredients for the meal. My grandfather had to be sure the boat was in top condition to take it out: Maintenance up to date, gas tank filled up, gauges working, and the anchor attached to the boat. The weather had to be checked to be sure it was a good day to go out. A lot of planning was involved. My grandparents did a lot of work behind the scene because they had a shared vision. A common interest. And they shared a common desire to create an amazing experience for the family visit. Time out on the water, enjoying a wonderful meal on a beautiful lake, with the people that meant the most to me in the world holds some of my best memories.

I would not have had that time with them if Nanny and Pop had not shared a vision, done the preparation necessary to make it happen and worked together toward a common goal. I am so thankful to them for being intentional with their lives in both their work and their play. They recognized the importance of playing together as a family. Those are values I want to live out and pass down in my own family. I do not know if ours will be on a houseboat, and I doubt my cooking will ever live up to my Nanny's, but I do know I'll be making some mean virgin pina coladas.

"Where there is no vision, the people perish" (Proverbs 29:18). You can get more specific:

- Where there is no vision, the family will perish
- Where there is no vision, your marriage will perish
- Where there is no vision, your dreams will perish

If you have nothing to look forward to, nothing to think about in order to motivate you through hard times, then your feelings will win, every time. That inner toddler's plea will convince you to order candy for breakfast. You will end up burnt out, malnourished and settling for a life out of a vending machine. Anything will do. You will not be concerned about the quality of the ingredients or the presentation of the meal. You will not even care about the astronomical price you are paying relative to what you get. You will be too ravished to notice. You will spend the last dollar in your pocket to buy something you don't even want because you are losing the war against your blood sugar levels. Your inner toddler wins again. Poor planning, poor results again, again and again. I'm sure you have heard the saying, "When you fail to plan, you plan to fail."

In the book Chazown[viii], Craig Groeschel writes:

"For the most part, people just stumble halfheartedly through life hoping tomorrow will be better than today. No plan. No dream. Mostly just existing. Hoping for a break. They just keep turning the pages of their life story, one after the other, until they get to the final chapter. And then…it's time for bed."

Isn't that what will happen if we are not careful? Life today is too rushed to think about tomorrow much less next week or next year or 30, 40, even 50 years from now. But you must. You must pause from today's emergencies long enough to make a plan for tomorrow or you will always just be surviving today's emergencies. Is that how you want to live? Do you want to just rush through your life and your marriage just surviving? Or do you want a happy, life-long marriage that is full of hope, commitment, vision and meaning?

Our team at iBloom is passionate about connecting women with their life purpose and helping them define their vision for their life and family. There are resources available at www.ibloom.us to help you create a clear vision for your life. Do not go another day just muddling through.

❖ Write your Dream List

A great exercise you can do to get you thinking forward is making a Dream List. This is a list of all of the things you want to do, places you want to see, people you want to serve, things you want to learn. It is putting the desires of your heart down on paper.

For some of us, this is easy. We know what we want. We have plenty of desires but just are not sure how or when they will ever materialize. For others, this is really hard. We have been running on adrenaline, putting out one fire after another for as long as we can remember. Dig deep. Think back to what you used to dream of when you were a child or of traditions you grew up with that you want to pass down to the next generation. Get away to a quiet place and just brainstorm.

If you find yourself completely stuck, then get out a pen and paper and write down all of the reasons you can not dream right now. Work pressure? Financial trouble? Wrong thinking? Lack of creativity? Take that list to God in prayer. Ask him to help you put all distractions out of your mind. Ask him to help you dream. God has given each and every one of us a unique purpose. He has given us desires in our hearts to help lead us to that unique purpose, the blueprint for your life. It may take some digging but be assured it is in there somewhere. Do not give up until you find it.

Now for your husband. I told you that I have a history of encouraging (nagging) my husband to do new things, to learn new things and do exercises just like this one. Well, I am older and wiser now. So I have learned to encourage without pressuring.

The way I got my husband started with his list was I took mine with me when we were heading out on a road trip to visit his parents. It is a 5 ½ hour drive, one way. About an hour into the trip, I asked him what he wanted to do before the year was up. His response, "I don't know." So I tried another question. If money were no object, what would you want to do next week? Now that got him rolling. In all fairness, I did give him the reality that I had not won the lottery. I just wanted to know what he wanted to do someday.

Starting the list was easy for him. He wanted to attend several sporting events, he wanted a leather recliner, he wanted to take a vacation, and he wanted to get a bigger television. I know, deep stuff.

But then it got a little harder. I asked him more details around each one. Who does he want to take with him to the sporting event, where does he want to go on vacation, what states or countries has he always wanted to visit?

When he started to get bored with the topic or said he wanted to check to see if he could hear the game on the radio, I complied. That was my clue that his interest in my "game" was up. Then while he was listening to the game, I worked a little more on my list. I matched up the parts of my list that coincided with his list to make an OUR list. His ideas inspired me with new ideas. I circled one that I thought might interest him, too. I put a note by the ones that I knew he would not enjoy, writing down who I might want to take with me. My grandmother, mom, sister, friend, daughter? The more specific I became with painting the picture of my vision for each item, the more excited I became! It made the trip to Illinois fly by. I did not even mind listening to sports radio for 3 hours. There is a first time for everything.

❖ Share Your Dream List

Why share your list? Why not just make your own list of dreams and then just let him figure his list out on his own? After all, after you have written your list and gotten excited about it, you have plenty to occupy your time without ever helping him. There are 2 main reasons it is important to share your Dream List with your husband.

First reason: intimacy. It will bring you closer together. I once heard a great definition of intimacy. Intimacy is allowing someone to do just that: In-To-Me-See. You become more intimate with someone when you allow them to get past the walls you put up with others, like peeling back the layers of the onion. You will have 5 categories of people in your life:

1. People who do not know anything about you.
2. People who know of you but who do not know you personally.
3. People you have met and who recognize you but have no personal relationship with you.

4. People you call friends/family. They have personal knowledge of you and you have personal knowledge of them.

5. Your spouse. That one special person that God has given you and has, through marriage, made you become one flesh.

If your friends know more about you than your spouse does, then you need to work on the intimacy in your relationship. I struggle with this one myself. My girlfriends are always so encouraging. They understand where I am coming from. They seem to always have my back. It is just easier to want to share with them than it is to share with my husband sometimes. God is showing me though that sharing my thoughts, my dreams and my fears with my spouse is vitally important to my marriage. He has gifted my husband and me differently for a purpose. My husband will raise concerns and opinions that my girlfriends do not, partly because he has a male perspective that I (and my girlfriends) do not have. He also has a vested interest in me and his opinion matters in our life together. We need to make decisions together. How are we supposed to make life plans together for a happy life-long marriage when he has no idea what I dream about, what I am afraid of or where I am insecure?

Being vulnerable is never easy. At first, it will feel like the first time of the season you head to the pool after a long winter in sweaters & Spanx[ix]. But after you dive in a few times, you will start to feel more and more comfortable. Bikini no... Tankini, yes.

Second reason: accountability. Ecclesiastes 4:9-10 says, "Two are better than one, because they have a good return for their work: if one falls down, his friend can help him up. But pity the man who falls and has no one to help him up."

When you have a partner who knows what you really want in life, he can help you keep your goals in focus. Men, by design, are hunters. They do not shop; they go in for the kill. Take advantage of this strength that God has instilled in your husband. Once he knows what you want to achieve, he can be tenacious in helping you get it.

When you are sharing your heart with your husband, he is better able to understand it. He can see where he can help make your dreams reality. You can be doing the same thing for him. It is a beautiful thing when you both begin to see past the dirty dishes and look forward into the dream kitchen; when you can see beyond the chores, the work and the sacrifice that must happen today in order for you to both realize your dreams for tomorrow.

❖ **Prioritize your goals**

So, do we pay off debt or buy a recliner? This is where it can get tricky. We moved this year and I started to get overwhelmed by the number of projects I wanted to complete in relation to the size of our project budget. It was clear after I made an extensive list, room by room, that this was going to require time and lots of patience.

Mike and I started to argue over what tasks were most important:

- What would get checked off of our list first?
- Where would the precious project money be spent?

Each item became a battle. I knew there had to be a better way to make our house a home. There had to be a way to remain friends with my husband while feathering our nest. But instead I wanted to storm out of the room and call him a bird brain. It was in this weak moment that I saw the wisdom in prioritizing our goals...BEFORE we were calling each other bird parts.

After we both cooled off, I grabbed my master list of all of the projects I had written down earlier. It was color-coded and broken down room by room. I know, I'm kind of a Martha Stewart/geek when it comes to this stuff. I also grabbed us something to drink and a snack. Food does wonders for making your husband cooperative.

I showed him my list and this did a few things:

- It showed Mike how much thought I had put into it already.
- It showed me that my way of doing it was completely clear to me but not to Mike...since I hadn't shared my list with him before.
- It showed us both that we were going to have to work together to prioritize or we were looking at a project list with the potential for an argument accompanying each and every item.

We decided to go through the list, item by item. I would label each with HIGH or LOW priority level and then he would label each item HIGH or LOW priority. Then we both take each of our HIGH lists and number them in order of importance. Then we compared lists. (I told you I could be a geek about this but bear with me.) Together we decided the top five projects we would do first. Now we have a plan. Now we both understand which projects did not make the cut. Now we both know that in order to make our way down our individual lists, we have to work together on the ones that are most important to both of us. No more hot-tempered debate, except for the occasional battle over paint colors.

What we did to plan our home improvement projects, you can do to plan your life together. Come to agreement on what is highest priority for you as a couple. Take the time to go over each of your lists. Understand why his HIGH list is his HIGH list. Share with him why your HIGH list is your HIGH list. See what things you both want to do and then come up with a plan together to make those dreams reality.

When you are working together toward a vision that you have both created together and prioritized together, it will be the glue that holds you together while you are in the prep-mode: when he is working extra hours to save up for your vacation, when you are taking the French class to be ready for your vacation to France and dinner has more French fries than home cooking. You will know you are giving up on something good, i.e. meatloaf and mashed potatoes, in order to get something greater in the end, a trip to France and the chance to practice your newly-learned language while you are there. Then you will not be feeling deprived of your husband's time while he is working overtime and he will not be aggravated because you're eating leftovers again. You are both sacrificing for each other for a common goal: Your Dream List.

❖ Help each other achieve them

If you do what we are talking about here, you will begin to see some amazing progress. You will:

- Experience a more intimate relationship with your husband.
- Identify your dreams, prioritize them and then make a plan for conquering them together.
- Provide accountability to each other and keep the vision in sight as a couple.

Now, how would you like to kick it up a notch? How would you like to take your marriage from good to great? Have your husband make the transition from thinking you are fine to thinking you are the most fabulous woman on the planet? I have two words for you: Help him.

It is great that you are at the point where you do not argue over what dream you will achieve first and when you are not complaining about the sacrifices you are both making to meet your goals. But what would happen if you went from negotiating for placement on the priority list to doing everything in your power to see all of his dreams come true during your lifetime, even the ones you could care less about. The ones you have ZERO interest in. What happens when you become willing to drop one of your HIGHs down to a LOW just so you can have the joy of seeing one of his dreams come true? Amazing is what happens. You have just graduated from inner-toddlerdom. You have now received a new "I'm making progress in sanctification" badge. You are now starting to think with the heart of Jesus.

Scripture says that God gives us more than we desire or can imagine (Ephesians 3:20). He sacrificed His life to give us what we did not even know we needed. He loved us without asking what was in it for Him. Learn to love your husband with the heart of Christ. The relationship you have with your husband should be the most intimate relationship you experience with another human. Ask God to show you how you can serve Him by serving your husband.

There are 5 categories for your Vision/Master Dream List as a couple:

1. Spiritual
2. Relational
3. Physical
4. Financial
5. Recreational

The couples that I have noticed who have the best relationships share the same vision, for the most part, in all or at least most of these categories. In order to enjoy the ideal marriage a couple would:

- Share the same faith
- Enjoy a deep commitment to each other and their family
- Be intentional in taking care of their bodies and get the proper amounts of rest, exercise and nutrition
- Be on the right track financially and agree on what to do with their money
- Value fun and know how to enjoy each other and their extended family

In short, they have a list, they have shared their list with each other and they are in agreement with the priority level of everything on their list. I am convinced that the more categories in which you share the vision with your spouse, the more connected you will be as a couple; the greater the prediction for success in your marriage; and the more likely you will be to not only finish the race together, but to finish it well. You will not just love each other; you will enjoy each other, all the while knowing that you are both in the same boat.

Chapter 5

Make Your Home a Safe Haven

"The wise woman builds up her home but the foolish woman tears it down with her own hands."

(Proverbs 14:1)

Writing with integrity is extremely important to me and that is why I have struggled with getting started with this topic. I have to confess that this is the toughest chapter for me to write. I have sat down to write it several times and found myself doing other projects that need attention. You know, the urgent stuff like laundry, email, locating the matches for the bag of solo socks I have collected in my laundry room. I am now recognizing the source of my procrastination.

Finally today I prayed, "God, who am I to offer advice on creating a safe haven? I do not have it figured out. I have laundry undone, a fridge that needs to be cleaned out and stocked back up. There's so much I still need to do. I haven't figured out how to keep the house clean and still sleep. I do not have enough patience with Halle Kate or Mike. We rush around in the mornings like crazy people getting off to work and preschool. My house is more chaotic than calm. Can't I write about something else? I have lots of girlfriends who are so much better at keeping their house in order than I am. Why am I the one writing this chapter? I'm not qualified!"

I think I heard Him tell me that I am not qualified to write anything in this book. No one is. Everyone is lacking in one area or in many areas. If perfection were a prerequisite for writing a book, or serving in a ministry, or teaching a subject, or being a spouse, or becoming a parent, or being a Christian, no one could do it. He urged me to clear off the Christmas cards from my kitchen counter, plop my laptop down and get to writing because this is a message He wants us to get. He wants YOU to get. He wants ME to get. We will never reach perfection in any area of our lives. He does not expect that of us. What He wants is for us to want to be more and more like Him... every day...in every way.

"OK God, you've made your point. I'll get to it."

So, especially with this chapter, know that I am sharing from one imperfect Christian gal to another, what God is teaching me. God is teaching me every day what to bring into and what to take out of my home. I am a remedial housekeeper. I am a cook-in-training. My organizational skills are improving day by day. I am just sharing with you what God is teaching me. I would not know these lessons if I had not required God's correction and instruction in the first place.

I have to also give credit to my family when it comes to the home front. They are amazing helpers around the house from cleaning the floors to cooking to laundry. Our dog sheds a ton and Mike is so good to sweep up all of the hair. He also does his fair share of cooking and laundry.

Halle Kate loves to help (most of the time) and wants to be doing what we are doing. She is also pretty darn good at cleaning the baseboards with wet wipes. Even our dog Chloe does her part by eating up all of the food that falls from the table. I am so thankful for all they do.

By nature I am a pack rat and Mike is a throw-it-outer. God knew what he was doing when he put us together. We take turns with most everything, helping each other to make our home a safe haven. A place we both long to return to each day. I invite you and your husband to join us on the journey to your own safe haven.

So how do we build up our home? How do we avoid tearing it down with our own hands? What is it that makes a house a home? What do you have to do to take it a step further and make your home into a safe haven? Let's take a closer look and see what these terms mean.

Home[x] is:
- one's place of residence
- domicile
- house
- the social unit formed by a family living together
- familiar or usual setting
- congenial environment
- the focus of one's domestic attention: *home is where the heart is*

Safe means:

- free from harm or risk: *unhurt*
- secure from threat of danger, harm, or loss
- successful at getting to a base in baseball without being put out
- affording safety or security from danger, risk, or difficulty
- obsolete of mental or moral faculties: *healthy, sound*
- not threatening danger: *harmless*
- unlikely to produce controversy or contradiction
- not likely to take risks: *cautious, trustworthy, reliable*

Haven is defined as:

- harbor, port
- a place of safety: *refuge*
- a place offering favorable opportunities or conditions: a haven for artists

A good working definition of Safe Haven would be: A place of residence offering a refuge from harm. A Safe Haven is a place where:

- You can relax
- You do not feel threatened

- You feel free to be yourself
- You enjoy and support each other as a family

It is, in fact, where your story begins…

But the reverse is also true. Your story will begin there even if your home is not a safe haven. When you do not feel comfortable or there are problems at home, you can begin your story feeling:

- Unloved
- Anxious
- Frazzled
- Misunderstood
- Like you have to be someone you are not
- In a word, miserable

You have to make decisions about what you want in your home. These are not just one-time decisions, but decisions which must be made every day and sometimes every hour. Do you want a safe haven or do you just want a house? Sometimes you will make a decision by doing, sometimes you will make a decision by refraining from doing. Sometimes it is in the words you say or the tone of your voice. Sometimes it is by the music you play or the scents in your home. More often than not, it will mostly be determined by your attitude. One day as I was driving through a nice neighborhood in Lexington, I was overcome with sadness when I made the divorce statistic personally relate to the street I was on. House after beautiful house— on the outside, that is. With a 50% divorce rate with first marriages and then an even higher divorce rate for second and third marriages, that meant that every other house was anything but a safe haven. On the outside all of the houses looked sturdy but the fact is, on the inside, over half of them were falling apart.

I have heard it said that children are like little mirrors. They reflect what they see in their parents. If you are frazzled and cranky, your children will be frazzled and cranky. If you are in a good mood, your children will be in a good mood. I think your home is a mirror, too. By being intentional in allowing your home to reflect the best of your family, this can serve you to actually become your best family.

Our goal is to build up, to take our home from being just a place of residence to being a secure, non-threatening refuge. We are not trying to measure up with Martha. We want what God wants for us: for our home to reflect the love, the coziness and the comfort of Christ, a place free from controversy, drama and risk. We want to create a safe harbor, not just for us, but also for our husbands, our families and our friends. A place we cannot wait to get back to each day. A place your husband is longing for in his heart. A place your children will someday want to invite their friends to come visit and that they will want to re-create when they have a home of their own one day. We want it to be a place where our best memories are made, where friends and family always want to visit...and leave within a reasonable time period. I'm just saying...

What do fish and house guests have in common? They both begin to stink after about three days.

That takes me back to our first topic...the importance of having house rules.

❖ Establish house rules for communicating

The first step from just having an address to living in an oasis is to establish some house rules. This is a very effective way to help everyone feel at ease. When we know what is expected, what is prohibited and what is encouraged, everyone breathes easier. Everyone can relax. No one is walking on eggshells or wondering about the mood of your home. You will have a steady, calm and comfortably-predictable environment that will act as a springboard for your life...your BEST life.

Allow little room for interpretation: For starters, you are not a mind reader and neither is anyone else. So talk about everything. Have family meetings. Post reminders of what you have agreed upon. The sooner you discuss who will do what, how you will do it, how often you will do it and what things are not acceptable under any circumstances, the better off you will be.

Create your own new normal: Let's take mealtime for example. Your husband may have grown up eating dinner while watching television. You may have always had family dinner around the dining room table with no television in sight. Your dad may have cooked and your mom may have cleaned up. Or your home may have been so frantic that you mostly ate in the car. Your history does not dictate your future.

You are a grown up now. This is your home and with that reality comes a lot of freedom and responsibility. You and your husband can choose to take bits and pieces of what you both grew up with or you may choose to scrap the old ways and start fresh with your own ways of doing things.

Be hands on: There is no cut and dry instruction manual for the right way to run your home. Homes have personalities, just like people. There are stuffy homes, there are comfy homes, there are creative homes, there are utilitarian homes, there are messy homes and there are tidy homes. There are laid back homes and uptight homes. It does not matter so much which personality you choose for your home so much as it matters that you and your husband are in agreement. Your home needs to be a haven for you and your spouse. You want to make it comfortable and inviting for you both. Do not be afraid to try new things until you find what works. Entertain his ideas even if you think they are silly. You both live there so it is more fun if you are both involved in the process. This will require some degree of compromise or you could end up living in a house suffering from split-personality syndrome.

Regardless of the personality you give your home, there are some proven guidelines for creating a safe haven you and your family will be proud to call home. Here are eight main building blocks:

1. *Eat together.* Mealtime is a time to connect with each other. Even if you cannot do it every day, make it a priority to do it as often as you can.

2. *Pray together.* Pray with and for your spouse. These will be some of your sweetest moments when you are interceding for one another in prayer.

3. *Love each other more than you love results.* Love who he is more than what he does or does not do for you. If he is slacking in an area, give him the benefit of the doubt; go above and beyond to show him you love him more than you love what he can do for you.

4. *Share highs/lows each day.* I know I mentioned this before but it is so important. Without making it somewhat routine to ask each other about the high and low of the day, you risk falling out of touch with your spouse. This allows you a quick way to stay connected and can really open up the conversation to what is most important to you and your spouse.

5. *Notice each other.* Do you give your dog a warmer greeting than you give your husband? I know I have accused my husband of doing that to me at our house. Each time you greet each other for the first time after

being away for a few hours think about the enthusiasm you would show your pet or that you would show when picking up your child from school. I know it sounds silly. But think about it. Your spouse deserves the excited look in your eyes, big hugs and genuine interest in what he did while he was away. It is easy to feel ignored by the people who are supposed to be closest to you. Make an effort to be sure your spouse does not feel invisible.

6. *Establish traditions together.* Making your own traditions and incorporating some from each of your families can be fun. They help you bond, as my sister Kelly would say. One quirky tradition my husband's family does is Pizza Hut pizza and shrimp cocktail on Christmas Eve. I know, it sounds so weird. When he was growing up, they would go to his Grandma Bea's house. She would order pizza and serve shrimp cocktail as an appetizer. They would share their big dinner on Christmas so it made it easy and kid friendly for them to do pizza and shrimp for Christmas Eve. In my family, Christmas Eve has always been our Big Day and then Christmas was a fun day of leftovers and visiting my paternal grandparents. My point is, what you think is normal; someone else may think is weird. The main point is to enjoy each other and to decide as a family what traditions you will establish in your home.

7. *Give thanks together.* I want my house to be a thankful house. We give thanks for meals, for getting rid of the dog's fleas, for clean underwear, for rain and sunshine

and snow. When we get grumpy around my house, Mike and Halle Kate know I will start asking them for their Ten Things. They have to share ten things for which they are thankful. I do not want my home to be full of grumbling and complaining. I want to cultivate grateful hearts. We may never get all we want, but we are confident that God has and will continue to supply all of our needs.

8. *Laugh...a lot.* Life is tough. If you do not laugh about things and learn to laugh at yourself then you are in for a serious, stressful and sad life. There is a time for everything. I think most of those times a little humor never hurt anyone. One of the best lessons I am teaching my daughter is how to see the humor in life. I do not want her to take herself so seriously that she can't laugh when she spills the milk. It's just milk, well that and whatever papers it soaked on my kitchen counter. We all make mistakes. Life is not perfect. Learn to roll with it and laugh, laugh and laugh some more. I want my home to be a jolly place.

❖ **Share a family calendar**

Lots of arguments could be avoided if more people would do this. I am still trying to figure out the best way to keep it updated, but it is hanging in our kitchen with the main stuff on it, so that's a start. My family is filled with the most important people in my life. My planner is a way to be sure that my schedule does not make a liar out of me.

Sit down with your hubbie and come to agreement on these things for starters:

- What night will you have a date night each week?
- Time for each other: It may not be sexy to schedule sex on your calendar but it sure beats never getting around to it.
- How many times your kiddos will spend the weekend with the grandparents?
- When you will be taking a vacation?
- How often you will be going to visit extended family?
- How often you have a girls' night and he can hang with the guys?

We also do Taco Tuesday (Mexican night) and Pizza Night most Fridays. We love both, so we have made it a part of our routine each week. Some weeks it is tacos and going out for pizza. Other weeks it is Mexican lasagna and frozen Red Baron (Tuscan style is our fave).

Cooking doesn't come easy for me. I've been known to catch the toaster on fire and set the smoke detector off many times in my cooking attempts. My sister Candice brings up the burning toaster story at just about every family gathering. I share my embarrassing story with you to encourage those of you who aren't naturals in the kitchen. Don't give up! Do your best to find recipes that you love. Recipes that are healthy and yummy! Your family needs your best, so don't worry about comparing yourself to others.

While we are on the topic of food, I have also made it a point to incorporate some of my mother-in-law's recipes on a regular basis. She has shared some great recipes that we love and Mike knows I am making a special effort for him when I fix his Mom's recipes. If you are cooking, you might as well earn bonus points. I should also mention that there are not nearly enough recipes that I can do as well as my Mom and Nanny. They are both GREAT cooks but don't measure a darn thing. It's like pulling teeth trying to replicate one of their dishes. I will not give up trying though because they are SO GOOD!!!

So whether it's a weekly pizza night, a family date night or taking a family walk after dinner, be consistent in planning to be together as a family. Communicate your schedules with each other, but most importantly, communicate how valuable it is for each of you to spend quality time together as a family.

Another little tidbit I learned recently is the "third object" phenomenon. I cannot remember where I learned this but communication happens more freely with the opposite sex when you are doing something together. Think about it. Girls can hang out at dinner and talk and talk and talk. We do not need props. You do not usually see a bunch of guys just sitting around talking to each other. They are out doing something together...watching sports, playing sports, running or whatever. So go for a walk with your husband and maybe he will talk to you. No promises, but it is worth a try.

❖ **Provide breathing room**

Too much togetherness can become too much. Allow each other some space in your safe haven. At our house, we each have our own zone. He has what we refer to as Headquarters (he may kill me for sharing that with the world. Not sure where that name came from but we have gone back and forth from calling it the Man Cave, the Man Den, Mike's Office and Headquarters. Headquarters is the most affectionate term). I have my office/craft room. I do most of my work from home and I am always doing projects so if we were ever going to be able to use our kitchen table for its intended purpose, then having my own work/craft place was pretty much a necessity.

We need space to have our stuff. I need a table that he will not be asking me to straighten up and he needs a place to retreat to watch a ballgame. I need a place to work where I am not distracted by the pile of laundry.

Not every family will have the space in their house for each person to have their own room. It may just be a favorite chair or a section of a room. Or it could just be space on the calendar where you can each do whatever you want and you promise each other to not interrupt or ask for help with something unless absolutely necessary. Do what you can to accommodate each other on having your own space.

We are having fun now trying for baby #2. We have agreed that if and when we get our second bundle, Mike will lose his office in order to set up a nursery and we will share my office/craft room. I am praying that God will soften Mike's heart to be satisfied with a new recliner instead. But I will share if I must.

❖ Be intentional about your surroundings

Now let's talk about some ideas for making your home look, feel and smell like a dream come true.

Did I already mention that I am a packrat? This one is tough for me. I am realizing that it is difficult to feel inspired and excited about life when there are lots of un-done projects staring me in the face. That it is incredibly difficult and frustrating to get ready in the morning when half of your clothes are still in the laundry room and the other half are dirty. One of the worst realizations is the whole "children are like mirrors" thing again. I hear myself telling Halle Kate to put her toys away when my own stuff is all over the place. God definitely has a creative method of teaching me.

God is a God of order and I want to be more like Him. Here are some tips that are helping me. Please share your favorite tips with me as well.

Tips for De-cluttering:

1. Keep a donate bag in each closet and one in the laundry room. Once a week or once a month, gather them up and drop them off at a donations center.

2. Before birthdays and Christmas, make a couple of walk-throughs of your house and look for things that do not meet these three criteria:

    a. Do we love it?

    b. Do we use it?

    c. Does it add beauty to our home?

3. If you still are not sure if you want to keep it, ask yourself, "If I did not already have this, would I buy it today knowing what I know now?"

Once you have de-cluttered, you and your family will feel lighter and less stressed. Brainstorm with your hubbie and dream of what would make your home a safe haven for you both.

On one of your date nights, stop at place that has a good variety of candle scents. Choose a fragrance you both love. You may decide to have a signature scent or you may choose to change your home's fragrance each season. We're vanilla at our house.

The main thing is to keep the conversation going. Hopefully you'll both agree with Dorothy that there really is no place like home.

Chapter 6
Play Together

So what's so important about playing together? Aren't we all grown up and have so many more important things to do? Yes and no. You are all grown up, but for this chapter that puts you at a disadvantage. Turns out, playing is child's play. Adults have to work at it. There is hope for you though. Learn some lessons from your niece, your friend's little one, or your own mini-me. All work and no play will make your marriage a dull marriage so find a way to work in some play.

Play: recreational activity; especially the spontaneous activity of children. I also found that play can be defined as "a move or series of moves calculated to arouse friendly feelings." You could say that in marriage it is important to make play by way of playing together.

Some may say you are being irresponsible to prioritize play into your marriage and they may even consider your behavior childish. That's great. If you can play like a child, you are a pro.

It amazes me how easy it is to go a day, a week, or even a month without having any fun. We feel so much pressure, both internally and externally, to "do" that we have forgotten how to just "be". Children do not have this problem, unless they have been forced to grow up too fast. They know to make their play urgent.

"Mommy, come play with me."

"OK, Halle Kate, just let me finish putting these groceries away first."

2 minutes later, while tugging on my pants...
"Mommy, you *said* you would play with me."

"I'll be right there. I just have to load the dishwasher and I'll play..."

1 minute later, which seems like a month in her 3 year old life, "Mommy, if you don't come play with me right now, I'm going to put you in time out!"

"OK, OK, you win. Let's go play!"

You see, kids get it. Playing is important. Playing is fun. It encourages creativity, relieves stress and facilitates bonding between the players. Playing is good. Sadly, as adults, it is now harder to set aside time to play than it was when we were children. But do not put it off. Make playing part of your day. Not just with your 3 year old but with your spouse. He may not be literally tugging at your pants for your attention or then again, maybe he does that more often than you would like (ha!). But either way, whether he realizes it or not, you both need to play together. Play as a couple and then also play as a family. Make playing a priority.

There are four main categories where you can learn to be intentional in playing with your spouse on a regular basis. Man that sounds boring. Sounds like a grown-up wrote it. My daughter would just say, "Mommy, go play with Daddy." That sounds less complicated, doesn't it?

Like any sport, you may feel a little awkward at first. You may feel like you do not have what it takes or that you are not any good at having fun together. Do not give up though. You and your husband are partners in life. You are all he gets. You cannot request a pinch hitter for this one. Do your best to be a great playmate. You may even find yourself having fun in the process.

- ❖ **On Dates**

This is one of my favorites: date night. This is a night you set aside each week to hang out together, just the two of you. Ideally, this would be away from kids and housework, but you can occasionally use those as props, if necessary. Date night is sacred in our house. Even with money being super tight right now, we are making it a priority and reaping the rewards in our relationship. This week we are in the middle of "Date Fest". This is a week full of date nights. Halle Kate is at Grandie's house all week. Thank God for Grandie (and Grandougie and Nanny, too. It does take a village).

In fact, looking back on our first year as parents, I don't think we would have preserved our sanity without date nights. Thanks to family and especially my sister Candice who lived near us. She was so wonderful to babysit and love on Halle Kate while we took much-needed time to ourselves! She really was a lifesaver and sanity preserver. If you have a Candice, be sure to let her know how much you appreciate her. If you don't have a Candice, don't be afraid to reach out for help from family and friends.

Parents need time with just grown ups and an occasional dinner at a restaurant that offers no kid's meal on the menu.

Date night is good. It reminds you of the reasons you are with this man you now call your husband. If you are like me, you sometimes end up referring to this guy in third person as your child's Daddy more than you do his real name or his nickname. Why do we do this? I have got to stop this because it is robbing me of part of the romantic desire I have for him. Referring to my husband as Daddy half the day and then trying to switch gears and call him my hottie husband at night can be a tough switch to make mentally. Let's make a pact to stop referring to our hunks as Daddy after 5pm.

While we are on the topic of names and such, I find myself referring to myself in 3rd person for no apparent reason when talking to my daughter. Why is this? I will say, "Mommy needs to go get something upstairs, or Mommy needs some quiet time or Mommy really needs a nap." Why do I feel I cannot say "I" most of the time? She knows I am her mother. Maybe it was the book, "Are You My Mother?"[xi] that makes me feel the need to constantly reinforce this for her. It could also be that when you are parenting a 3 year old it is easy to feel some confusion at times over who is in charge.

OK, where was I... Oh, the importance of date night. Another benefit of date night: it will preserve your sanity and keep you from rambling on about things that are not relevant.

It is extremely, I repeat, extremely important to schedule in date nights. These nights will not just miraculously occur. They take planning and effort, but they are well worth it. Spend time writing down some of the things you used to do when you were dating. If you have forgotten how to play, pick up one of those coupon books which give you tons of ideas of what to do with your adult selves. Ask your friends for suggestions. If you are too worn out to leave the house or if you come up dry while brainstorming, then let your first date be snuggling on the couch for a much-needed nap. Spooning recommended, but not required.

Make it a habit to peruse your town's newspaper or look online to see what is happening in your area. There may be some free things that would be fun, something on your dream list that you can tackle, or just a restaurant you have both wanted to visit. While you are sans children, you could offer to be a Candice to your friends/family members with little ones still at home. It can be a fun date night for you, great practice if you want to be parents someday, and a HUGE blessing to the ones you are serving.

It does not matter so much what you do on your date night. It is that you have that night together…consistently… and that you take time for each other. It is on date night that you remind yourselves each week of your vision as a couple. You reinforce your anchor and that will help you to brave the waves that come at you during the following week.

❖ While Working

You may not be able to drop all responsibilities and be on date night for an entire week. Work is part of life. You may both have challenging jobs, handle the responsibilities of your home, raising children and/or pets; you may be some of those super-human people who also manage to care for elderly parents. You are doing all of this while being active in Church and giving blood regularly. Life is tough!

The way I see it, you can spend your days lamenting over how tough your life is or you can give thanks to God for each day of your life. Thank God for your husband and that you have someone with whom to share life's responsibilities. In other words, it does not cost any more to find joy in each day. I heard on a radio program recently that you can choose to whine or you can choose to worship, but you cannot do both at the same time.

When it comes to marriage, I think you can apply that by choosing to pick at your spouse or by choosing to give thanks for your spouse. You can choose to work together as a team or you can choose to tear each other down. I hope you will choose to work together toward your common vision which includes playing together while you work. Here are some suggestions to get you started:

- Have a reward waiting after you finish a project together.
- Encourage each other in the tasks you do while you are apart. Celebrate each other's successes.

- Review your vision at the beginning of each week. This helps to keep the main things the main things.
- Put notes in his jacket pocket or on his steering wheel. Let him know you will miss him while he's away or let him know you have a surprise waiting for him when he gets home.

Ask your husband how you can pray for him as he leaves for work. Pray that God would show you ways to incorporate fun into the work that needs to be done. You may have heard the quote, "Do something you love and you will never work a day in your life." Well, I am not suggesting that we will ever love laundry or cleaning necessarily, but I do know that we serve a mighty God who is more than able to give us a proper perspective when it comes to our work.

We may not love doing piles of laundry, but we can be praying for those loved ones that we are doing laundry for...thanking God for each person as we serve them with our time. We may never get pleasure out of cleaning a bathroom. If you do, you need to ventilate the bathroom. Those chemicals are getting to you, Sister... but we can be thankful for our home and the indoor plumbing and we can pray for those who would love the opportunity to clean their own bathroom.

I know I am starting to sound like your mother when she wanted you to eat all of your carrots, "There are starving children in Africa. Finish your dinner." Well as tired as we may be of those words, there are still starving people in our world. In fact, as I write this there are approximately 1 billion people facing starvation.

We will choose to whine or we will choose to worship. Part of nurturing a playful spirit is cultivating a grateful heart. When you are grateful, you can manage to have fun even while doing the mundane chores of life. You can play together even while there is still much work to be done. It is all a matter of perspective.

❖ At Home

We all know those people who live for Friday. You may even be one of those people, but I hope not. Those are the people who start the countdown on Monday to just make it through until Friday.

- Monday, "Oh no, it's Monday. I cannot possibly enjoy even a minute of it."
- Tuesday, "At least we're a day closer to hump day."
- Wednesday, "Good, I've survived until Wednesday, almost over the hump to get to that golden day. Oh, how I wish it were Friday."
- Thursday, "Friday Eve…can it get here any faster?"
- Friday, "Now I can enjoy myself. Well, not until 5:00, but I can almost enjoy myself."
- Saturday & Sunday, I've got nothing for you. These are the people I don't spend my weekends with so I have no idea what they speak of on these days.

Are you living for Friday? Are you only allowing yourself to enjoy life on certain days or while you are on vacation or once you have children or after the laundry is finished or when your children are in college or when you have finally completed everything on your to-do list? If so, you are going to have a lot of sad moments, days, seasons and years. Monday comprises 1/7th of your entire life. If you live to be 90 years old, 12.8 years of your life will be spent on Mondays. If you sleep an average of 7 hours a night...ok, my head is hurting from trying to calculate it. Let's just say that a lot of your life is spent asleep. Fair enough? Asleep!

7 hours is almost a third of your whole day. You are living on a Monday for 12.8 years and then you are asleep for longer than Tuesday & Wednesday combined. I do not point this out to depress you, but to drive home a point. The majority of time that you and your husband (and the rest of your family) spend together will be at home. This time is limited. This time is precious. Do what you can to make it enjoyable. Do everything in your power to make home a place where you have fun together and you enjoy life and you enjoy each other.

This is a day the Lord has made, let us rejoice and be glad in it (Psalm 118:24). The enemy will do everything possible to make you miserable during those precious moments from when you both wake up until you part for the day. He will be waiting at the door to do it again the moment you are united. "Sin is crouching at your door; it desires to have you but you must master it" (Genesis 4:7).

The enemy wants strife. He wants arguments. He does not want you to have fun in your house. He comes to steal, kill and destroy (John 10:10). If you want to make that snake madder than a bull, have fun in your house.

- ❖ **In Bed**

There are three kinds of love in relationships[xii]: lust, romantic love and long-term commitment.

#1 Lust: I want sex, lots and lots of sex.

#2 Romantic love: This is crazy, seemingly drug-induced love projected upon a particular person. It has been likened to the manic phase of someone suffering from manic depression.

#3 Long-term attachment: The "mature" stage. Where you experience comfort, calm, security and you feel united with this person.

I think an ideal marriage would be heavy on #3, wrapped in #2, and then sprinkled with a healthy dash of #1. We need it all to keep things fresh in marriage. No, you are not a hormone-crazed teenager, but you need to do what lovers do in order to feel what lovers feel. I have mentioned many times the fickle nature of our pesky feelings. Your feelings will tell you:

- "You're too tired to play."
- "There's no time to play."

- "You don't like to play."
- "Why should you have to add Recreation Director to your already too-long list of responsibilities?"
- "Sex is necessary to produce children but it is not fun."
- "You don't need sex...you need a nap."
- "It's his job to bring in the romance and to be creative in bed."
- "What has he done to deserve sex? If he does _____ then, and only then, does he get sex."

You can listen to your feelings and choose to tear down your home and your bed. Or you can choose to remain stagnant and just comply to a boring sex life with your spouse. Or you can choose to build up your marriage by being an active participant in your love life. You can apply the same planning and creativity you use to do scrapbooking or photography or to piece together the perfect outfit. You can use the problem solving ability you are praised for at work to find ways to incorporate play in your personal life.

Where are you giving the majority of your energy? If you are too tired or busy to have sex with your spouse then you are too tired and/or too busy. There are different kinds of tired, too. Here are a few:

1. Just had a baby tired
2. Working 2 ½ jobs tired

3. Stayed up too late on Facebook tired

If it is #1 tired, I hear you, Sister. But keep in mind that you may be facing this kind of tired for a while...a long while. Wait the time-frame suggested by your doctor (If your doctor is male I suggest adding another week or two...ha!) Do not keep sex off limits for too long though. Compared to the restfulness you experienced before you were a parent, you will always be tired...always. So, go ahead and have tired sex. It is better than no sex.

If you are #2 tired, I'm right there with you. Evaluate why you are working so hard. Do you have a vision for getting out of debt? Are you pursuing a dream? Do you have a plan to one day only have 1 job? Keep that vision in mind and still take time to enjoy each other. Are there things other family members can help you with to give you a break? Look for ways you can conserve your energy so you will have some left for play. You are tired, there is no disputing that, but keep the love alive so that when you realize your vision as a couple, you are still a couple. Do not put your love life on hold while you are working crazy schedules. You are working to support each other, to support your family. The jobs are to serve you and your family...not the other way around.

If you are #3 tired, you certainly are not alone. I think computers and televisions are the biggest obstacles to couples enjoying amazing sex lives. We get on Facebook just to send one message or to see the latest pictures of our friends' children and before we know it, 3 hours of our life is gone, kaput, never to be lived again. The enemy will rationalize this as, "You have worked so hard, you need the human connection. You have only talked to your 3 year old today and your husband is watching football. You deserve this virtual social hour and you need it to preserve your sanity."

Facebook is great, but like anything else, the enemy can and will use it to destroy your life, if you let him. Anything in excess is harmful. A friend of mine uses a timer. She sets it for thirty minutes and when the timer goes off, she shuts down the computer: email, Facebook, internet surfing, etc. She masters her time and does not allow it to become an issue. If you are spending hours on social networks and your own family network is suffering, husband included, then consider an internet fast or using a timer. I do not think we logon with the intent of tearing down our marriages, but it can happen. So be intentional in building your own personal firewall to protect your marriage and your family. The new pictures of your friends' kids can wait.

Give your best to your spouse and your family. Pray that God will give you everything you need to do your job well, maintain friendships, and get the rest your body needs. He designed our day to include 24 hours. God wants you to do what can be accomplished within that time frame and do it well, without feeling exhausted or beaten or like a failure at the end of the day. Ask Him to prioritize your to-do list. I will tell you right now that having sex with your husband is up there on the priority list.

Give Him your reservations about it. Give Him all of the reasons you are not doing it. Tell Him all of the reasons you do not have time for your husband. Then take time to listen to what He has to say about it. He will advise you. He will help you streamline the rest of your day. He will give you better rest and help you to fall asleep quicker. He can help you choose the perfect outfit on the first try in the morning. He can even encourage your husband to do his own laundry and fix dinner. I am talking from experience ladies.

A wonderful mentor of mine often says that, "When you take care of what is important to God, God will take care of what is important to you." If you are afraid that if you give energy and time to your spouse you will have nothing left for yourself, then there are two things wrong with that line of thinking. First, you are making your decision from a state of fear which we are instructed not to do (2 Timothy 1:7). Second, you are forgetting that God's math and our math are not equal. On our level, when we give something away, we are left with less than we started with. When God is in the picture, when we choose to give, He blesses us with more than we started with. Remember the little boy who gave his lunch to Jesus for the sake of the crowd? He could have kept it. He must have been hungry. There was no guarantee he would even get a bite of it. But in faith, he selflessly gave what he had and left the result up to Jesus. The result? The multitude was fed and there were 12 basketfuls leftover after everyone was satisfied. Not after everyone had a small snack, but after each and every family of the five thousand had eaten to the point of being satisfied.

Be willing to share what you have with Jesus and serve your husband both in and out of the bedroom. Do not make decisions out of fear or a scarcity mentality. You and your husband are to enjoy each other. Sex is one of the greatest gifts in life. Ask God to multiply it in your marriage and ask Him to help you both know what to do so that you both are satisfied. Neither of you feeling used or ignored, but completely satisfied in each other's arms.

You will not find that satisfaction at work. You will not experience that level of intimacy with your friends or family. God has reserved that unique physical, emotional and spiritual gift for marriage. Be grateful for that gift. Serve each other, even when you are tired. If you are just working sex into your life, but not enjoying it, then take the time and attention necessary to solve that problem. God gave you your spouse to enjoy, both in and out of the bedroom.

Chapter 7
Be a United Front

In the dedication for this book, I told of Nehemiah and his heart to rebuild the wall of Jerusalem. I see a strong parallel between the physical wall of Jerusalem and the symbolic wall that is the union of marriage. Our "marriage wall" is not strong enough in our country, in my house, or in your house. It needs serious rebuilding, strengthening and guarding against attack.

Our country's marriage wall is in shambles. There are huge gaping holes in it and it is wide open for attack. My marriage wall is stronger than it used to be, but still requires daily attention and guarding. Only you and your husband know the state of your marriage wall. I would challenge you to do a close inspection and do what is necessary to make repairs and build it strong enough to endure your lifetime.

My marriage wall started off pretty shaky. It was not secure, it had structural issues and it was not being guarded properly. When I got married I did not know my wall was in such bad shape. Heck, I did not even know I needed a marriage wall. Much less that I needed to build it tall and strong or that it had vulnerable places from my insecurities and past failures in relationships. I did not know all that I did not know. So I was relying on what I thought was right, what my friends told me and luck. This did not make for a strong wall.

Be a United Front

I am now learning what it takes to build a strong marriage wall. One that will support us, protect us and give us clear boundaries to live within. God is faithful in showing me what needs to be done, but not in an overwhelming way. I am convinced that if He showed me everything that needed to be done all at once, I would give up before I even got started. He is faithful to show us where we need to be working and He will never just leave us on our own to figure it out by ourselves. But whether we choose to do things by trial and error or by reading the instructions, it is up to us.

He will not force us to do things His way. He gives us the choice every time; whether we will choose to build up or tear down; whether it concerns our marriage or just the everyday decisions of our lives. In your house, you may have a strong wall or you may be standing there, naked, with no wall at all. You may just now be realizing the need for your own marriage wall. You may feel vulnerable right now. Like your enemy is unclear. You may feel like you are under attack, not just by the enemy, but by your own spouse or family. You may be feeling confused about what boundaries you need to set for your marriage.

Whether your marriage wall resembles the rubble that Nehemiah grieved over or the strong wall that they brought to completion, going forward in your marriage as a united front, is the only way to strengthen and preserve your marriage. Define your enemy and define your allies and then constantly remind yourselves who's who. Often I will say to Mike when he is getting frustrated over something and is seemingly taking it out on me, "Hey, we are on the same team here. I want the best for you. How can I help?" Your husband is your ally. God is your ally. People or things or activities that would want to tear down your marriage are your enemies.

> "'For this reason a man will leave his father and mother and be united to his wife, and the two will become one flesh'? So they are no longer two, but one. Therefore what God has joined together, let man not separate" (Matthew 19:5-6).

I have a heart to help rebuild marriages…to start fresh from the rubble. Whether that rubble is the result of what we have inherited or what we have managed to destroy ourselves is not the point. Our marriage walls are broken and they need rebuilding. We must recognize the wrecking balls that got us to this point: the brokenness, the failed relationships, the wrong expectations, the broken homes you may have come from, the divorces you may have witnessed or that you perhaps even experienced yourself. We must take them to God's feet and leave them there along with any excuses we may be tempted to keep. Do not hold on to the old, but move forward with the new.

> "Therefore, if anyone is in Christ, he is a new creation: the old has gone, the new has come!" (2 Corinthians 5:17).

Whether you know it or not, when you accepted Christ as your Savior, He made all things new. You are a new creation. Sometimes we want to hold onto the old as a child would to a nasty, worn and tattered security blanket. Why? Because it is what we know. It may be worn out, smelly, torn and does not fit us anymore, but we think we still need it. Well, the truth is, you don't. Let go of your smelly-security-blanket-old-ways of doing things and allow God to show you His way of doing things. Not just in marriage, but in all areas of your life. You are made new. He will give you all you need to fully live out your new identity in Christ both in your marriage and in your life.

I, like Nehemiah, want to start fresh. I want to burn my old, wrong ways of doing things, and with God's help, build a strong wall of protection around my marriage. I want to assist you as you build your own marriage wall. I want to be a co-laborer with all believers in building up a strong marriage wall around the sanctity of marriage as a whole in our country. I know I cannot do it alone; I need each of you to participate. I need God working in every detail. I need lots of marriage prayer warriors all over the world praying for a strengthening of marriage.

Each time we choose to build up our homes rather than tear down, when we choose to act meekly, exercising strength under control, when we choose to react in love rather than how our inner-toddler wants us to, we are building our wall. Brick by brick, decision by decision, prayer by prayer, we are strengthening our marriage wall.

Marriage is viewed by the majority as being disposable today. When Christian marriages look no different than secular marriage, we have two big problems: First, lots of Christian couples still running around with their stinking security blankets, not realizing that they are new creations in Christ. Second, countless number of non-believers making decisions, based on what they have seen happen to Christian couples: that being a Christian does not have much, if any impact, on whether marriages fail or flourish. The Christian and non-Christian seem to reason that if the first husband does not work out, don't worry, you can always try again. Spouses are not meant to be disposable. For many though, instead of until death do us part it has become:

- until debt do us part
- until sickness do us part
- until irreconcilable differences do us part

What does irreconcilable differences mean anyway? When it boils down to it, those couples never claimed their new identity as a married couple. They were still operating as two separate entities, but were joined together by name and address.

Yes, our marriage walls are weak; weak in foundation, in protection and in durability. There is not a magic prayer for marriage. No 100% money-back guarantee. Building your marriage wall will not be easy, but it is absolutely worth the effort.

Here's a glimpse of what it took for Nehemiah and his helpers…

> "So I stationed armed guards at the most vulnerable places of the wall and assigned people by families with their swords, lances, and bows. After looking things over I stood up and spoke to the nobles, officials, and everyone else. 'Don't be afraid of them. Put your minds on the Master, great and awesome, and then fight for your brothers, your sons, your daughters, your wives, and your homes.'…
>
> 'The common laborers held a tool in one hand and a spear in the other. Each of the builders had a sword strapped to his side as he worked. I kept the trumpeter at my side to sound the alert" (Nehemiah 4:13-14, &18).
>
> "The wall was finished on the twenty-fifth day of Elul. It had taken fifty-two days. When all our enemies heard the news and all the surrounding nations saw it, our enemies totally lost their nerve. They knew that God was behind the work." (Nehemiah 6:15-16).

Just like Nehemiah and his fellow builders, for you to have a happy, life-long marriage, you will have to roll up your sleeves and grab a tool in one hand and a spear in the other. It will take work, a common vision, prayer, stamina and last but not least, a firm and steady determination that you are on the same team, working together to complete a great work.

You absolutely must have a united front in marriage. Not just when you feel like it, not only when you get your way, and not only when it is the popular thing to do. Stay focused and determined in discerning the difference between your allies and your enemies and you will prevail. You will build a strong wall of protection around your marriage. You will finish strong as a couple. You can do it. Because just like with Jerusalem, God is on your side and others will know it. He will be glorified through your building up and your obedience in refusing to tear down. You will do it all, not by your own strength or might, but by the strength of Christ at work in you (Philippians 2:13, TNIV).

So, what is required for you to build the marriage wall together? How do you become and remain a united front?

❖ You must communicate

Just as Nehemiah had assigned people at different stations and had a trumpeter at the ready to sound the alert, you will need to communicate with each other, with God and with trusted counsel. You will do this in many ways, but here are some conversation starters:

- Share your best and worst each night. My family does this during dinner. This will get you in the habit of discussing more than the weather. If you both go to bed knowing the best thing and the worst thing you encountered each day, then you are keeping intimacy alive. It will also be a laser approach to talking about what matters most to each of you.

- Ask how you can pray for one another each morning. This is an amazing way to remind you both that you are in fact on the same team. To know that your spouse knows what you are struggling with or are concerned about and is praying on your behalf is a huge deposit in your marriage.

- Be willing to seek reinforcement. Make a pact that if either of you starts to feel your marriage slipping, or if you are not sure how to move forward to make progress in your marriage, you will seek counsel from your Church or from a Christian counselor or coach. Visit www.findchristiancounselor.com for trusted resources.

- Spend daily time in prayer. The only one who can bring about change, strengthen your marriage and work constantly on your behalf is Jesus. Take time to communicate with Him. Take time to share your heart with Him and then take time to listen to His response, correction and instruction. Oh, and then of course, apply it to your life…that is usually the hardest part, right?

❖ **Recognize scripture's instruction: WE not, "YOU and ME"**

"And the two will become one flesh. So they are no longer two but one" (Mark 10:8).

Post it everywhere if necessary: No longer two but one. Not fully making this transition after getting married can be one of the worst offenders in marriage. Just as you are a new creation in Christ when you become a Christian, God makes you and your husband a new creation through marriage. He joins you together as one flesh. It is the couples who do not claim their new identity that are in for, at best, a rough road or, at worst, a dead end.

They are still desperately clinging to their old ways of doing things; both holding tightly to their smelly security blankets. They are looking out for their "me needs" instead of what is best for them both. They choose to do their own thing rather than working together in decision making, priority setting and time managing. They are chipping away at their marriage wall with each decision made as a "me" instead of as a "we."

Why do we have trouble making the transition from two to one in our decision making? I know when I make poor decisions, it is usually for these reasons: fear, selfishness, uncertainty and lack of faith. I am afraid that if I do not look out for myself, no one will. I am uncertain that my husband will appreciate or even notice the sacrifice I made for him. Or I just do not have faith that blessings follow obedience. I do not trust God's promises enough to do what he instructs me to do. Simple as that. We can make lots of excuses, but I am certain that most of our selfish decisions in marriage are a result of fear and/or lack of faith.

❖ Come to a decision together, then own it

Marriage is full of choices. How many children? Where will you live? How often will you go on vacation? Where will you go on vacation? How will you pay for vacation? (Can you tell I'm dreaming of a vacation?) When will you retire? How much should you save for retirement? How will you parent? Who will pay the bills? And on and on and on...

It is important that you discuss each of these "opportunities to choose" together, that you make a decision together and that you both own that decision by sticking by it. Yes, there will be times you will need to make revisions to your previous decisions. There will be times for you to come together and evaluate what is working and what is not working. There is not a time, however, to change your plan in the middle of a play without discussing it with each other first. Once you have decided something together, as much as humanly possible, you need to stick to that decision until you can discuss it further and agree on a revision together.

A major ingredient in marriage is accountability. You will help each other stay on track when one of you wants to quit or take the easy way out. You will remind each other of the vision you have for your marriage and your life. You will encourage each other to press on toward the "something great" you have envisioned together rather than allowing yourselves to settle for just "something good" along the way. You need each other. You also need to know that you can trust the other person to be faithful to your plan. This applies in:

- Finances
- Parenting
- Managing your household
- Planning for retirement
- Time management

The more time you spend discussing things in anticipation of what is to come, the better prepared and unified you will be for those events. To finish strong it will require you both being united in coming to decisions, as well as, sticking to your decisions.

❖ Have a "blind respect" for each other

"Don't worry; I've got your back!" Doesn't it feel great to hear that? Wouldn't it feel wonderful to know that your friends and family always have your back? That they are looking out for you, protecting you, preserving your reputation and nipping any gossip about you in the bud? This is hopefully true for you. I hope that you can trust your friends and family to always believe the best about you and not say things behind your back that they would not feel comfortable saying while you were in the room with them.

Have you heard the expression, "I can talk about my sister, but you better not!"? Well, I think it is on the right track, but still flawed. It means I can say things about my sister when she aggravates me, but if you talk badly about her, I will defend her, so watch out. Well, no one should be talking badly about this girl in the first place, but there is a

Be a United Front

defensiveness we have in regards to our family. This defensiveness should be at its peak when concerning our spouse.

Many companies have what I refer to as a "Complain Up" policy. This means that they do not allow gossip to run loose in their organization. If you work for Dave Ramsey[xiii], for example, you would actually be fired for it. He just will not tolerate it. His belief, in a nutshell, is that if you have a complaint against someone, then you should address it with that person or with management. In other words, do not talk badly about the person or situation with someone who has no power or authority to bring about resolution. Brilliant.

Isn't that a great policy to have for your life? If you are upset with someone, especially your spouse, do not call your girlfriends or even your well-meaning mother. Talk to your husband, a counselor, or pray about the situation. I may have mentioned it before, but this is a good spot to remind you. When you find yourself upset, or angry, or feeling misunderstood, go to the throne instead of the phone (unknown). Make this a policy in your marriage. Whatever you do, refuse to allow yourself to slander your spouse. If you do, you are talking badly of yourself (remember the One Flesh?) and you are dividing yourselves...with witnesses.

Be able to rest in confidence that your spouse will talk to you if he has an issue, not to his buddies. Allow him the security that you are speaking well of him and that he can trust you with his heart. There is no room in marriage for doubting if your spouse really has your back. It should be a given.

Whether it comes to financial decisions or parenting decisions or whatever the topic may be, choose to have a "blind respect" for each other. Even if you do not know why he said or did something, always give him your support. Always offer him the benefit of the doubt in front of others. He deserves your respect. This is especially important when it comes to parenting children. If your children see any wiggle room in your parenting decisions, they will play into it every time. Instead, if they know that what Mom says, Dad supports and what Dad says, Mom supports then you are both in for a much more enjoyable parenting experience.

My grandmother told me that was one of the things that she and my grandfather were most proud of as parents...deciding ahead of time that they would respect each other's decisions in that way. When you are both parenting from the same page, you are raising more confident children and saving yourselves a lot of headaches. Your children will know that their parents are in agreement with each other. They will feel secure and they will not be taught how to manipulate people and situations just to get what they want. I know there are lots and lots of lessons I want to teach my children. How to manipulate others is not one of those lessons.

A question to ask your spouse often, to keep your marriage wall strong, is surprisingly simple, "What can I do for you?" I know it can be a scary question to ask sometimes. The enemy will all but convince you that you do not have time to stop what you are doing to help your husband. Do not listen to that nonsense. You will find that the things your husband wants help with are not huge daunting tasks.

I know Mike's requests are usually to return something to somewhere or someone, make a phone call, or his favorite and most asked…rub his feet. I am pretty sure that if I would just rub his feet each night, he would believe I was the best wife on the planet. OK, maybe I would need to rub more than his feet… But still, do not be afraid to ask your spouse that magic question, "What can I do for you?" Expect God to give you all you need to follow through and believe in faith that your marriage will be blessed as a result.

Conclusion

Do you want to a happy marriage? You may think that is a silly question. You bought the book. You are reading it. But that does not answer the question. In John Chapter 5, Jesus met a man at the pools of Bethesda, a man who had been disabled for over 38 years. He had been lying by the pools which were believed to have healing powers. When the water in the pool would stir, disabled people would enter the pool in hope of healing. This man had no one to help him into the water. So day after day, year after year he had just been laying there by the pool. Jesus comes to Him and shows compassion, but before helping him, he asks, "Do you want to get well?" The man starts in on how bleak his circumstances are…that he had no one there to help him. He was whining and understandably so. He had been disabled for 38 years… Jesus told him to "Get up! Pick up your mat and walk." At once the man was cured and he got up and walked away for the first time in 38 years.

Marriage in our country is sick and diseased. We have mishandled it for so long as a society that we do not know what a good, healthy marriage even looks like. We have seen countless marriages fail, we have seen marriages lived out in such a worldly way that we almost have given up on a healthy marriage the way God designed it. It may seem almost easier to have a lame marriage than to get our hopes up that we could have a vibrant, life-long, lasting, and yes, even happy marriage. Jesus wants us to let go of our excuses and to trust Him enough to act on His instructions for marriage. No resource, no book, no pool of Bethesda is going to help your marriage unless you take action doing what Jesus instructs you to do. Get up, pick up your mat, and walk!

Be encouraged that God wants your marriage to be anything but mediocre. Marriage should be a safe place for each of you to enjoy each other, serve each other and support each other. If you have landed in a mediocre marriage, do not panic. There is hope as long as you are both still breathing. Start implementing what you have learned and watch your marriage move from mediocre to amazing.

In marriage and in life it is important to follow Stephen Covey's suggestion and begin with the end in mind. I believe that everyone does this whether they recognize it or not. They begin their day believing positive things will happen to them that day or believing that negative things will happen to them that day. Henry Ford said, "Whether a man believes he can or believes he can't, he's right." Now I am not suggesting that anyone gets married and begins a countdown to divorce. What I am suggesting is that successful Christian marriages begin each day, each choice, each word and each anniversary with the end (mostly) in mind. They believe that God is able to sustain their life and their marriage. They are not spending time or energy debating on divorce as an option. They are resolute in believing that they are going to devote themselves to one another. Could something go wrong? Yes. Could they end up getting divorced down the line anyway? Yes. I recently read an interview where a woman was sharing her advice based on 55 years of marriage. She said you must not ever entertain the possibility of divorce as a couple. When asked if she had ever gotten so angry or frustrated with her husband that she considered it, she said, "Divorce? No. Murder, many times…" You will get angry with each other. You will disappoint each other. But establish early on that you are stuck with each other. Divorce is not in your vocabulary.

I recently spoke with a dear friend of mine who is going through a devastating divorce. She devoted herself to this man for 30 years and then all of a sudden, he wanted out of the marriage. She was sucker punched. They had raised 2 beautiful children, enjoyed life together and even mentored other younger couples in marriage. To say that she was shocked would be a massive understatement. I asked her, as gently as I could, what she would change if anything about the way she had given herself to her marriage and to him. Her answer: nothing. She would change nothing. What good would it have done to have given herself partially or to have spent all of their time together during those 30 years waiting for something bad to happen. Would it have helped to live each day of her marriage expecting a divorce? No, it would have stolen away her joy over the 30 years.

The bottom line is we cannot control other people, especially not our spouses. We have to rely on God completely. We have to entrust God with our marriage much the same way parents must entrust their children to God. We do not hold our marriage loosely, but we hold tightly to

God knowing that He is holding every detail, every circumstance and every day of our lives in the palm of His hand. We then act on what we know. We walk in obedience with Him, trusting Him with our story. We do not know every decision that our spouse will ever make. We do not even know every decision that WE will make. What we do know is that today God has called us to love our neighbor as ourselves. Our spouse is both. Our spouse is in a separate, neighboring physical body, but is also, spiritually, the same flesh. I know that God wants us to get this right on more than one level.

Two things to leave you with:

1. Begin each day with your spouse with the end in mind. Have and hold your vision for your marriage close to your heart. This will make all decisions along the way so much easier.

2. When you are not sure what to do, ALWAYS choose love. Jesus has already given us the answer that is the right answer for any and all multiple choice questions. Choose love. Depend on Him to show you what love looks like in your situation. Sometimes love is tough and sometimes it is sacrificial. Ask Him for wisdom to know the difference. He will show you every time.

My Happy Marriage Action Plan

What is your ONE TAKEAWAY from **Chapter 1**?

Ask God to help you **Avoid Expectations** by choosing **one** bullet point and taking action...
- ☐ Check your attitude
- ☐ Show your gratitude
- ☐ Avoid comparisons
- ☐ Practice humility

What is the ONE THING you are going to do before moving on to Chapter 2?

What is your ONE TAKEAWAY from **Chapter 2**?

Ask God to help you **Serve One Another** by choosing **one** bullet point and taking action.
- ☐ You go first...don't wait for him to make the first move
- ☐ Pray for your spouse, asking God how you can help
- ☐ Ask your spouse what you can do for him
- ☐ Don't keep score

What is the ONE THING you are going to do before moving on to Chapter 3?

What is your ONE TAKEAWAY from **Chapter 3**?

Ask God to help you **Remember To Be Friends First** by choosing **one** bullet point and taking action:
- ☐ Encourage
- ☐ Listen
- ☐ Take up for him
- ☐ Enjoy

What is the ONE THING you are going to do before moving on to Chapter 4?

What is your ONE TAKEAWAY from **Chapter 4**?

Ask God to help you **Share a Vision** with your mate by choosing **one** bullet point and taking action:
- ☐ Write your dream list
- ☐ Share your dream list
- ☐ Prioritize your goals
- ☐ Help each other achieve them

What is the ONE THING you are going to do before moving on to Chapter 5?

What is your ONE TAKEAWAY from **Chapter 5**?

Ask God to help **Make Your Home a Safe Haven** by choosing **one** bullet point and taking action:
- ☐ Establish house rules for communicating
- ☐ Share a family calendar
- ☐ Provide breathing room
- ☐ Be intentional about your surroundings

What is the ONE THING you are going to do before moving on to Chapter 6?

What is your ONE TAKEAWAY from **Chapter 6**?

Ask God to inspire you to **Play Together** by choosing **one** bullet point and taking action:
- ☐ On Dates
- ☐ While working
- ☐ At Home
- ☐ In Bed

What is the ONE THING you are going to do before moving on to Chapter 7?

What is your ONE TAKEAWAY from **Chapter 7**?

Ask for God to show you how to **Be a United Front** by choosing **one** bullet point and taking action:
- ☐ You must communicate
- ☐ Recognize scripture's instruction: WE, not "YOU and ME"
- ☐ Come to a decision, then own it
- ☐ Have a "blind respect" for each other

What is the ONE THING you are going to do before putting this book in a predominant place on your bookshelf and/or ordering lots of copies for your friends?

I would love to hear about your successes! Go to www.leighannnapier.com/hmstories and share your story.

Looking for more Happy Marriage Resources?

Often, my coaching clients know what they want but just aren't sure how to get there. Others just know that they will get there much faster with the accountability and encouragement of a coach. They've read the books, been to the conferences, and have the t-shirt but they get stuck when it comes to applying it to their own marriage. Well, if that describes you, if you have trouble turning information into transformation, check out the resources on the Happy Marriage website.

Start your Happy Marriage adventure by checking out my blog at http://leighannnapier.com/blog

You'll find:

- a place where you'll be encouraged and you can share your story by commenting

- information on the Happy Marriage Coaching Program and other things to come under the "upcoming events" tab

- and lastly, you can contact me if you have any questions or if you just aren't finding what you are looking for

I would be honored to be your coach as you journey toward your very own happy, life-long marriage.

Endnotes

[i] John Trent, *Breaking the Cycle of Divorce* (Focus On the Family, 2006)

[ii] www.listen.org

[iii] www.ibloom.us

[iv] Michael Z, www.thewisdomoftherooms.com

[v] [http://www.merriam-webster.com]

[vi] [www.listen.org]

[vii] James Dobson, *Focus On the Family Column*, June 2004

[viii] Craig Groeschel, *Chazown-A Different Way To See Your Life* (Multnomah, 2006)

[ix] [http://www.spanx.com/home/index.jsp]

[x] [http://www.merriam-webster.com]

[xi] P.D. Eastman, *Are You My Mother?*, (HarperCollins Children's Books, 1998)

[xii] The Economist (Feb 12, 2004)

[xiii] [www.daveramsey.com]

iBloom is your go-to place for Christian Life Coaching for Women! We exist to inspire and empower every woman on the planet to live a life she loves (and a life that honors God)!

iBloom offers the following for women:

Individual Life Coaching

Group Life Coaching

Motivational Speakers

Special Events

Resources to equip YOU

Plus, much more!

For more information, visit us at www.ibloom.us.

Other Ways to Get Connected with iBloom:

Email – info@ibloom.us
Facebook – www.ibloom.us/facebook
Twitter – www.twitter.com/ibloom

www.ingramcontent.com/pod-product-compliance
Lightning Source LLC
LaVergne TN
LVHW041629070426
835507LV00008B/530